STRAiGHT
Expectations

of related interest

Transitioning Together
One Couple's Journey of Gender and Identity Discovery
Wenn B. Lawson and Beatrice M. Lawson
ISBN 978 1 78592 103 2
eISBN 978 1 78450 365 9

Trans Voices
Becoming Who You Are
Declan Henry
Foreword by Professor Stephen Whittle, OBE
Afterword by Jane Fae
ISBN 978 1 78592 240 4
eISBN 978 1 78450 520 2

STRAIGHT
Expectations

THE STORY OF A FAMILY IN TRANSITION

PEGGY CRYDEN, LMFT

With Janet E. Goldstein-Ball, LMFT

Jessica Kingsley *Publishers*
London and Philadelphia

First published in 2017
by Jessica Kingsley Publishers
73 Collier Street
London N1 9BE, UK
and
400 Market Street, Suite 400
Philadelphia, PA 19106, USA

www.jkp.com

Library of Congress Cataloging in Publication Data
Title: Straight expectations : the story of a family in transition / Peggy
Cryden.
Description: London ; Philadelphia : Jessica Kingsley Publishers, 2017. |
Includes bibliographical references.
Identifiers: LCCN 2016058920 (print) | LCCN 2017015143 (ebook) |
ISBN
9781784505370 (ebook) | ISBN 9781785927485 (alk. paper)
Subjects: LCSH: Cryden, Peggy. | Parents of gays--United States--Biography. |
Parents of transgender children--United States--Biography. | Gays--Family
relationships--United States. | Transgender people--Family
relationships--United States. | Families--United States.
Classification: LCC HQ759.9145 (ebook) | LCC HQ759.9145 .C79 2017
(print) |
DDC 306.874086/7--dc23

British Library Cataloguing in Publication Data
A CIP catalogue record for this book is available from the British Library

ISBN 978 1 78592 748 5
eISBN 978 1 78450 537 0

Printed and bound in Great Britain

Thank you to the three most amazing men in my life: my husband and my two incredibly courageous, brilliant and loving sons. You inspire me and make me proud every day. I love you!

CONTENTS

EDITOR'S NOTE

This book is written from a mother's perspective. In staying true to the story as it unfolded, we felt it was important to use gender pronouns reflecting Peggy's experience at the time, rather than the reality of Jake's essential male identity. I hope readers will understand and accommodate the reason for this unusual usage.

This is something Peggy experiences on a daily basis. Her memories are like a split screen. When thinking about Jake before the transition, the automatic memories are of him as Julia. After the transition they are of Jake. This is reflected in the book by the flexible use of pronouns, depending on the chronology of the story.

"I think a lot of parents in my shoes would agree. You cannot erase the years of memory or replace them. They are written in our brains and we see it that way. I honor my child, but I also have to honor my memories."

Peggy Cryden, LMFT

PREFACE

I first met Peggy Cryden 12 years ago when I was invited to join a women's poker group hosted by a mutual friend. Peggy was one of three women in the group who had changed careers mid-life to become marriage and family therapists. The group also included two psychologists, and a few other women who worked in different fields. I was at a time in my life when my enthusiasm for the job I'd been doing in the entertainment business for the past 15 years was waning. Psychology had always been an interest and I have these women to thank for influencing me to go back to school and pursue a career in counseling.

The poker games were hosted by different members and were held every three or four weeks. During the games held at Peggy's house I had the opportunity to get to know her family. They seemed warm and friendly, and also like a pretty normal middle-class Jewish family living in Los Angeles. Peggy's daughter Julia would always come over to the table to say hello and chat for a few minutes. She seemed like an affable teenager, outgoing and enthusiastic about life. Julia was a musician who played the drums in a band. A couple of us went to see her perform at a club and were impressed by her talent. She had a tomboyish, punk rocker sort of look. I later learned that Julia was a lesbian. Peggy was completely accepting of that fact and supported her daughter whole-heartedly. We all let Julia into our hearts and in some cases, our homes, as she baby-sat for a few of our children. Little did we know what was actually going on with this very likable teenage girl.

At one of the poker games Peggy hosted a year or so later, a couple of us noticed a change in Julia's appearance. She was dressed like a boy, with her hair cut in a more masculine style. Her voice seemed lower. I noticed that she seemed to be growing sideburns. I saw the other women in the group nervously glancing around, also wondering what was going on with Peggy's daughter. A few days later I asked the organizer about Julia. She was one of Peggy's closest friends and told me that Julia was transgender, taking hormones, and about to have surgery. Word must have gotten back to Peggy and, at the next game, she explained the situation to all of us. We learned that Julia had felt she was supposed to be a boy from the time she was three. As a teenager, she had been struggling to find her identity. At first, she believed she was a lesbian, but that didn't feel right. What Julia wanted was to be a man.

When Julia started having suicidal thoughts, Peggy got her into a program at Children's Hospital in Los Angeles for transgender youth. After two years of attending various modes of therapy, a physician had finally given the okay for Julia to go ahead with gender affirming surgery. At this very moment, Julia was in the process of becoming Jake. We were all moved by

Peggy's open-minded attitude and complete support of her oldest child.

But Peggy's story is not only about raising a transgender child. During the time she was dealing with her teenager's gender identity crisis, Peggy was also struggling with her own identity issues. During a wine tasting party we both attended, I learned that she had been adopted as a baby and had recently concluded a long search for her birth mother, which resulted in their reunification after 46 years. Later, after Peggy and I became hiking buddies, she confided that she had faced many difficult challenges while being raised by her adoptive parents. In addition, I learned that her younger child Jay had been struggling with an eating disorder and obsessive compulsive disorder (OCD) since he was 14 years old. Yet Peggy's story is not all heartache. Despite everything she has experienced, she is an extremely warm, humorous, intelligent woman with an infectious zest for life. Moreover, the journey Peggy has been on so far has helped her form her parenting skills and her own unique philosophy of life, which is summed up in her family motto—"It is what it is."

During one of our hikes in the canyon, Peggy told me she wanted to write a book about herself and her family, chronicling the obstacles they had all faced and overcome on their path to healing, and what she had learned in the process. She confided that she had struggled most of her life with attention deficit hyperactivity disorder (ADHD), and didn't think she could write the memoir on her own. I had a background in writing and editing, and had the goal of writing a book myself related to my new field. All I needed was a good topic, and here was one being handed to me on a silver platter. I proposed to Peggy that we write the book together and she leapt at the idea.

This book is an opportunity for Peggy to tell her fascinating story. It is also an opportunity to educate the reader about gender dysphoria, a psychological diagnosis that affects 0.3 percent of the population, though this number is potentially higher due to the proportion of people who are reluctant to disclose their gender identity.[1] Life can be agonizing for those who feel they were "born in the wrong body," which coincidentally is the name of the MSNBC documentary that featured Jake. Peggy, Jake, and Jay have also appeared several times on *The Oprah Winfrey Show*. Their story is unusual in that it has a happy ending.

This is a tale many parents can relate to, about having children who did not turn out the way they had imagined or hoped. Peggy's story encourages us to be open-minded about our children's choices and needs, and to be loving and supportive even if those choices and needs are difficult for us to digest. However, this does not mean we should support choices that will endanger our children or cause them to get in trouble with the law. Peggy's decisions regarding her children's welfare were not made lightly. They were made after much research, much discussion, much consultation, and many hours of therapy, and they were decisions

---

1   Gates, G.J. (2011) *How Many People Are Lesbian, Gay, Bisexual, and Transgender?* Los Angeles, CA: Williams Institute, UCLA School of Law.

that saved both her sons' lives and kept the family from disintegrating. Peggy's journey will help educate the reader about the transgender experience and other LGBTQ issues, is meaningful for parents, and gives much food for thought about identity, sprinkled throughout with her humorous contemplations about the human condition.

Janet E. Goldstein-Ball, LMFT

1

THE GREEN ROOM

—— (September 2007) ——

My son Jake and I tried to control our excitement and act like professionals as we waited in the green room. But, as I sat there on the couch with my 16-year-old boy, I started to wonder if I was doing the right thing. My husband had expressed reservations about exposing our son on national television. He was concerned about his safety. I became fearful that there could be dangerous people out there who might cause harm to Jake after seeing him on the show. He had been tormented enough already by the bullies at his high school. I suddenly felt compelled to engage him in an open and honest way about the possible consequences of this TV appearance. But Jake did not waver from his conviction that he needed to do this. Always a champion of the underdog, my son felt that if someone didn't speak out about the struggles of being a transgender person, then his community would continue to live in fear, never have equal rights or be understood. Instead, they would always be in jeopardy. Jake convinced me that we had to take this risk. I assured him I would stand beside him and protect him as much as I could.

A producer from MSNBC contacted us while Jake was attending a program for transgender teens at Children's Hospital in Los Angeles. That led to our first media appearance, in the MSNBC documentary *Born in the Wrong Body*. After it aired, I suspected we might be contacted by a talk show since this topic was becoming hot in the media at that time. I remember telling Jake, "If anybody ever wants us to appear on a talk show, the only one I would consider would be *Oprah*." I felt she would handle our situation with respect. The first talk show to contact us was Montel Williams. I didn't know his show that well and my intuition told me it wasn't the right outlet for us. I jokingly told Jake, "I'm passing on Montel. We are holding out for *Oprah*." A week or so later, as the universe would have it, her producers called. After a phone interview, they agreed that Jake would be an interesting guest. They thought our story was unique because it had, and continues to have, a positive outcome.

Before I knew what hit us, we were on a plane to Chicago. We received the red carpet treatment as soon as we got off the airplane. A limousine took us to our hotel to freshen up, then rushed us directly to Harpo Studios for a wardrobe fitting. My son, who usually wore a black tee-shirt, jeans and tennis shoes, was offered three beautiful designer outfits. Jake looked so handsome in his choice of a gray button-down shirt, black slacks, and Oxford shoes. He cleaned up nicely!

Back at the hotel that night we were almost too excited and nervous to sleep. We were picked up early the next day by another limousine. We arrived at the studio and went through a strict security check.

Staff members escorted us into the green room, which was lovely. It was fully stocked with delicious food and drinks for us to snack on. They treated us like stars and attended to our every need. A producer came in and told us what would be happening. Jake was dressed in the outfit he had picked the day before and I was wearing an outfit I brought from home. Oh, by the way, this was at 7:00 a.m. I thought to myself, "How are they going to make me look camera-ready at 7:00 in the morning? No one looks good this early." Luckily a gifted makeup person came in and airbrushed my face with professional broadcast cosmetics. I glanced in the mirror and couldn't believe how fabulous I looked.

We sat a little while collecting ourselves, waiting to be escorted to the stage and watching as the show began on a monitor. They finally announced us, and a crew member came in to get us. It was show time! As we walked in, a clapping audience greeted us. The moment was surreal, walking by all those people, about to bare our souls. The lights were bright. For a moment, it felt overwhelming. They sat me in the front row of the audience and Jake went up on stage to sit with Oprah. He looked so confident and comfortable in the limelight. My motherly pride took over. I was beaming, looking at my cute son, as the taping began. Oprah did her introduction, then played a short clip of us at home that they had taped a couple weeks prior.

When I look back at how we wound up in the green room and appearing on the show, it seems so insignificant compared to all of the events in our lives that led to Oprah's interest in our story. It was a rollercoaster ride that had its ups and downs, and began the day I was born. Everything I experienced taught me not to have inflexible "straight" expectations. If our expectations are rigid, it makes it difficult to accept and embrace whatever life throws our way, and is not conducive to raising emotionally healthy kids. Straight and narrow thinking prevents us from loving our children unconditionally and fully appreciating everything that makes them who they are.

2

RAISED BY WOLVES

—————— (Early 1960s) ——————

In order to understand why it was so miraculous that I developed the skills to raise healthy children who are now productive members of society, when it all could have gone horribly wrong, I would like to take you back and paint a picture of my upbringing. The neighborhood I grew up in was a typical 1960s middle-class community in West Los Angeles. Flat streets with cookie-cutter track homes, bicycles in the front yard. A park up the street where the children played, schools we all walked to. Dads went to work, moms stayed home. Friendly milkmen made deliveries in the morning. In the afternoon we'd hear the jingle of the ice cream truck driving by while kids played in the street.

On the outside it all looked quite normal, and for most of the families in the neighborhood it probably was. Except for ours. The worst thing in those days was to be the family that was different, the family that others whispered about. The family with the disheveled mother who escorted her embarrassed son and daughter to the camp bus in a bathrobe, the mother who took the pet cat for walks, the mother who, in her shirt-maker dress and heels, was found on the front lawn in a catatonic state.

Here's my family portrait. My older brother and I were both adopted as infants (but are not related by blood) by a middle-class Reform Jewish married couple. My adopted father Joe was 12 years older than my adopted mother Joan. In fact, my father was already 40 when he married my mother, which was very unusual in those days. We weren't adopted until he was in his late 40s. I always feared that people would assume my father was my grandfather. Dad was of the generation that believed young children should be quiet and only speak when spoken to. He was an astrophysicist who was very successful, revered in his field, and immersed in his work. Mom was a teacher who taught adults English as a second language during the day and at night. When she was away in the evenings, dad was left to supervise, which basically meant we were left to fend for ourselves. He'd sit in the living room absorbed in his books, oblivious to what we were up to. It's a wonder we didn't poke an eye out or set the house on fire.

Joan and Joe appeared to have a "normal" middle-class adult life. They had friends, went out for meals, traveled all over the world, had season tickets at the Music Center, and relaxed at the yacht club on the weekends. Joan was a painter, took classes at a well-known art institute, and volunteered as a docent at the art museum. She had a few women friends, mostly the wives of my father's acquaintances.

It always surprised me that my mother was able to put herself together, get to work on time, and perform well at her job. Yet she couldn't perform the simplest domestic chores at home. To this day I still don't know if she simply didn't want to do these chores or just wasn't capable. Either way, the message was still the same to me as a child: that mom didn't care. For instance, she would send my brother and me to school with psychotic, inedible lunches. A typical sandwich would be a piece of leftover cooked chicken, still on the bone, slapped between two pieces of white bread, with a hunk of wet lettuce and a slice of worm-eaten tomato. Or, even better, her infamous peanut butter with yellow mustard and wet lettuce. The *pièce de résistance* was her tuna sandwich. She would dump a can of tuna packed in oil (people weren't as healthy in those days), undrained, on white bread, and top it off with the obligatory wet lettuce. The fish smell was overwhelming. I'm surprised it didn't drive my friends away. The sandwiches were loosely wrapped in wax paper (plastic sandwich bags were still a few years away) and tossed in a paper bag, with a huge mealy apple and a few crumbled chocolate chip cookies smashed beneath the apple.

On the way to school, my lunch bag would get soggy and break. I'd leave a trail of food on the sidewalk and wind up at school with no lunch. The stray pets in the neighborhood were getting fat, but I was still hungry. Thus began my life of petty crime. Joe kept spare change in the drawer of his desk in his home office. I would sneak in there and steal 35 cents to pay for a hot lunch from the school cafeteria. My instinct to survive this chaotic, neglectful upbringing made me very resourceful. Eventually I managed to get a job in the cafeteria wrapping the silverware in napkins and this entitled me to a free lunch.

It was difficult for mom to get out of bed in the morning until she had taken her morning pill to counteract the effect of the tranquilizer she had taken the night before. Since dad had already left for work, we were on our own from a very young age getting ready for school. Like most kids in that era, we walked to and from school every day, rain or shine. I remember a funny incident that happened one day when a friend and I were walking home from school in the pouring rain. We stepped off the curb and waded through the flooded gutter. As we walked out of the water, my friend noticed she had lost one of her penny loafers. We laughed as it floated down into the sewer. I was glad it wasn't my shoe going down the gutter, because I never would have heard the end of how careless and irresponsible I was, and how I should have used my "noggin" and worn my galoshes. This was only one of the typical comments I often heard growing up. I also regularly heard, "If your head wasn't screwed onto your shoulders, you would lose it," and, "You don't use the sense you were born with." Even though we might find these statements humorous as adults, this type of constant berating can have a devastating effect on a child's self-esteem.

Growing up with my mother Joan was a lot like growing up with an alcoholic parent. She never created a nurturing, safe environment for us. After school and the completion of our homework, my brother and I would join up with local kids and play a game of hide-and-seek, "over-the-line," or ride our bikes until it was time to go home for dinner. We would walk into the house and typically find mom lying on the couch, complaining of a headache or backache. We knew dinner was ready by the smell of charred broccoli.

My mother had zero interest or passion for cooking, thus she never learned how to prepare a decent meal. She was famous for serving us horribly burned dinners. For instance, she would take frozen hamburger patties directly out of the freezer, toss them in a frying pan, and crank up the heat. Then she'd toss instant white rice (a new product in those days) and a package of frozen broccoli into separate pans, and put the flame on high. After that, she'd assume her usual reclined position on the couch. My brother and I would walk in the house, take a whiff and shout, "Mom! Something is burning!" She'd reply, "Oh, I guess dinner is ready." It took me many years to learn that hamburgers were not supposed to be black on the outside and gray in the middle.

If I were lucky, I'd get invited to my playmate Virginia's house for dinner. I was always excited when I went to her house, because her mother would make us perfectly cooked hamburgers and crisp, yummy tater tots. I remember sitting at their kitchen table and being served what seemed at the time like the most amazing gourmet meal. It probably wasn't that great, but it was a heck of a lot better than what I got at home. Out of necessity, my brother and I both became pretty good cooks. It was either learn for ourselves or be destined to a life of "PB&J" sandwiches.

Our family meals pleasantly changed after my dad brought home one of the first microwave ovens. Since mom had no idea how to operate it, she was forced to follow the cookbook that came with it. After that, she was able to prepare food that was almost normal and somewhat tasty. When our house was burglarized, a few months following the purchase, one of the items taken was the microwave. Dad, who had graciously never complained about the burned dinners, ran out and replaced it immediately. He was no fool; he knew when he had a good thing going.

I knew there was something odd about my mother, however it wasn't until I became a therapist that I realized how truly ill she was. If she were a client, I would diagnose her with borderline personality disorder, bulimia nervosa, major depressive disorder, and extreme anxiety, which explains most of her behavior. I remember the embarrassment of being with her in the supermarket as a child and watching her polish off entire boxes of chocolate chip cookies or six-packs of ice cream bars by the time we reached the check-out stand. I've never forgotten the puzzled looks on the cashiers' faces as my mother set down the near-empty boxes on the counter. As a child, I had no comprehension of how sick this behavior was. I just hoped there would be one last cookie left for me by the time we got home.

Dad's job as an aerospace engineer and duties as a reserve captain in the United States Navy required him to travel quite a bit. He also joined every club imaginable and volunteered to write every newsletter, from the neighborhood monthly to the yacht club quarterly. As a result, he wasn't much of a hands-on parent. He didn't play sports with my brother, although he did make one feeble attempt at being a baseball coach. He was a genius and a highly intellectual man who spent most of his time in his head. Even though he had many friends and was very sociable, it was really hard for us to connect with him on an emotional level. Neither he nor my mother was adept at physical or verbal expressions of love.

Dad was gone a lot and sometimes I questioned if his absence was deliberate, his method of coping with my mother. I'm sure he felt she was in good hands—she went to a psychiatrist two or three times a week and had an extensive personal home pharmacy, which she tapped into on a daily basis. I think he believed he had done all he could for her. But what about us? To this day it dumbfounds me to think that dad felt it was okay to leave us alone with her. Here was a man who was brilliant and accomplished, but he was oblivious to how his wife's erratic behavior was negatively affecting his children.

The neighbors knew my mother was odd, but they didn't know the extent of it. They didn't know about her extreme lack of self-esteem and mood instability, which created such self-doubt that she would question and recount everything she said or did in her interpersonal interactions in order to find validation. I would come home, overhear her having a conversation, and wonder if she had company. But then I realized it was just mom talking to herself, again. It's not unusual to occasionally talk to one's self, but she would engage in full-on, two-sided conversations. She was always preparing conversations to have with her psychiatrist, or reviewing interactions with her girlfriends because she was insecure that she might embarrass herself or had already embarrassed herself. She was always looking for reassurance that she had said the right thing.

My mother was also paranoid that people didn't like her and were making plans behind her back. I might overhear her saying something like, "When I talked to Sheila the other day, I suggested we ride together to go to the play. She told me she was coming from somewhere else and didn't have time to pick me up. It made me think that maybe she didn't want to be alone in the car with me for that long. However, she seemed to have time to pick up Donna, which makes me angry." She believed everyone was plotting against her, didn't like her and was treating her unkindly.

These conversations were just one more weird thing about mom. Not only did she talk to herself, but, when a thought popped into her head, she would obsessively scramble to find any scrap of paper available to write it down so she wouldn't forget to discuss that issue with her psychiatrist. I'd find pieces of paper everywhere— notebook paper, a paper napkin, a scrap of a shopping bag—with incoherent, random thoughts scribbled all over them. Her wallet was swollen with notes she crammed into it for safekeeping.

The other mothers in the neighborhood appeared to have it more together. They were sociable, fashionable, and more personable. My mother alienated herself from others by being awkward and negative. In retrospect, I now realize she was really shy and intimidated by confident people, and didn't know how to handle herself. She just couldn't function well in social situations. I think part of her knew she was different. She could tell other women in the neighborhood treated her condescendingly. She couldn't regulate her emotions and often acted out in rage or jealousy. Her behavior was usually inappropriate for the situation, but she didn't seem to care. She made a point of teaching us the rules of etiquette, but somehow they didn't seem to apply to her. Even though she knew it was not polite in company to pick up one's dessert plate and lick it clean, she still would.

The friends mom made through dad's social circle treated her like she was a teenager and walked on eggshells around her. They loved my dad and felt sorry for her. She tried to do things with girlfriends, but her inability to be flexible and tolerate change made her anxious when plans would not go her way. The anxiety shortened her temper and she would lash out. Her favorite line was, "Dammit to hell!" She was so afraid of being abandoned by people that she avoided even trying to connect. If a connection were to occur, her belief that abandonment was inevitable would cause her to subconsciously sabotage the friendship in order to avoid the pain of another loss. She was a beautiful woman, but lived in both physical and emotional pain almost her entire life.

Joan's overwhelming insecurity and her inability to emotionally regulate created anxiety so extreme that it often led to panic attacks. She once got overwhelmed and had a panic attack while looking at mattresses at Macy's Department Store. She lay down for a moment on a display bed to collect herself. A salesperson saw her and assumed she had passed out. The paramedics were called. Joan sat up, startled by all the commotion, not realizing at first that all the fuss was over her. Embarrassed, she explained, "I had a bad reaction to some medication I am taking. I was feeling a little dizzy and needed to lay down for a moment."

I also remember a time years later, when my brother and I were adults, enjoying a day in the park with our families. Our kids were playing on the slide then moved on to another area. Suddenly one of my children approached me and said, "Is grandma okay?" I replied, "Why do you ask?" My younger son Jay turned and pointed. I looked and saw my mother lying on the slide, face up with her eyes closed, and her arms crossed over her chest. She looked as if she were posed for her own funeral. The children were startled and asked, "Is grandma dead?" Because we were so used to grandma's bizarre behavior, instead of panicking, we all broke out in laughter and the kids took pictures. We approached to see if she was truly okay and discovered she was just taking a nap.

I remember another time when my brother and I and our families had taken my mother out to dinner at an Italian restaurant in our neighborhood. As we were exiting the restaurant after a lovely meal, I looked down and noticed that my mother was only wearing one shoe. Controlling myself from laughing, I calmly asked, "Mom, where is your other shoe?" She replied, "What do you mean? I'm not wearing it? Oh, so that's why my foot felt so comfortable!" My brother went back and found the missing shoe under the table. Because of all we had experienced with her, we had to find the humor in these situations. My brother had the shoe wrapped in a "to-go" box, brought it to her and said, "Here's your leftovers, mom." Even she couldn't control herself from laughing. As crazy as she was, she still had a good sense of humor and could laugh when she wasn't shrouded in depression.

When I was very young, I remember coming home and finding Joan sitting on the front lawn staring into space. I thought it was odd that she would be sitting on the grass in a dress and heels, but because I was such a young child, I dismissed it. Our neighbor Marge told me Joan had been pulling weeds. Twenty years later, Marge told me the truth: my mother had become overwhelmed with anxiety, had an emotional breakdown, and was literally unable to get up on her own. Our housekeeper Willa cared for her until dad could make it home.

As a therapist, I was curious to know what could have contributed to my mother's emotional instability. According to what I was told about her upbringing, she was the oldest child and the apple of my grandfather's eye until her younger brother and sister were born. After that, she felt like she'd been abandoned and neglected by her father. At that time her father was an accomplished lawyer and had high expectations for all of his children. For some reason, she felt like she could never measure up. She was very bright but her insecurities got in the way of her development and she never fully achieved what she probably could have. Her mother was rarely at home. She was off doing her part for the war effort and being a socialite. A tragedy occurred when my mother's brother, who became the favored child, went swimming and contracted polio at age 16. He became partially paralyzed and contracted encephalitis, which caused schizophrenia. I believe the more constant care that my uncle required from my grandmother led to my mother and her younger sister feeling horribly abandoned.

As an adult, my mother had surgery for a chronic back condition. While in the hospital, she was given a pain medication that she was allergic to, which caused her to hallucinate. That frightened her to such a degree that she had one of her first psychotic episodes. Four months after marrying my father, she became pregnant. At seven months' gestation, she suffered a particularly gruesome late-term miscarriage of a baby boy and had to have a life-saving emergency hysterectomy at 28 years old, the reason why my brother and I were adopted. The horror of the miscarriage along with the heartbreak of losing a child, as well as losing the ability to ever have more biological children, were major factors in the further decline of her emotional stability.

My brother and I never felt close to our parents. I recall saying to myself, "If I ever have kids, I want my family to be different." (Little did I know at the time just *how* different my family would be!) I wanted to be present for my children and to be involved in their lives. I had an idealized vision of what a family should be. As a child I dreamed of having a mother who would be my mentor, who would bond with me in that special female way that a healthy mother bonds with her daughter and teach me how to be a proud and productive woman. Joan's inability to form close emotional connections made it virtually impossible for her to create intimate bonds with anyone. Sadly, for both of us, she was never able to be a positive influence in my life.

You might wonder after hearing about my upbringing how I wound up a fairly well-adjusted adult and competent parent. Research shows that a child needs at least one important person in their life who gives them love and nurturing. This person doesn't have to be a family member. It can be a family friend, a neighbor, a teacher, a coach, a religious figure, a housekeeper, or a caregiver. Research shows that a child needs at least one significant person in their life who is loving and nurturing. Having this important person in their life contributes to the child developing into a resilient, well-adjusted human being. In my life I was lucky enough to have three women who fulfilled this role for me. They were my grandmother Margaret, our housekeeper Willa, and our next-door neighbor Marge.

3

SAVED
BY THE BELLES

— (Early 1960s–1974) —

GRANDMA MARGARET

My adoptive maternal grandmother Margaret was the first positive female relation and role model in my life. She was a well-mannered, even-tempered, proper woman. Her hair was perfectly coiffed, her clothes beautifully tailored, and she always looked fashionable and lovely. She favored long skirts and never wore pants due to her self-consciousness about her bowlegs. I always knew by the way she dressed and carried herself that she was a proud woman. I admired how patient she was with grandpa, who was older and hard of hearing, and her mentally disabled adult son (my uncle) who also lived with her. I never heard her complain about anything.

Grandma Margaret was a socialite and also quite a humanitarian. She was a role model for independent women. Grandma was a true matriarch who was at the wheel of our metaphorical family car. During World War II, while grandpa Joe was working as a prominent lawyer, she contributed to the war effort by driving servicemen around in a double-clutch army jeep. This influenced her driving for years to come. I remember when we were young and she used to drive us places. Even though her car at that time had an automatic transmission, she still drove double-footed, with one foot on the gas and the other on the brake. I used to get nauseated driving with her, with all the jerky stops and accelerations. The moment I got my driver's license, I took over the driving duties. "Let me be your chauffeur," I offered. I'd pick grandma up on Sundays and we'd go to lunch at the elegant Bullocks Wilshire department store. Those outings were a treat and the type of thing my mother and I rarely did together.

Grandma was a pretty "hip" lady who always had my back. I often wondered if she had been a bit on the wild side when she was young, and if that was something we had in common in addition to our first names. Margaret, affectionately called Margie by friends and family, loved to throw parties, which is another great characteristic I adopted from her. She hosted all the holiday celebrations. I fondly recall the gatherings at her house with all our relatives and close family friends. We'd get together at Thanksgiving and Christmas. She would make an amazing meal, with help from her housekeeper Willa. My mouth still waters when I think of her incredibly juicy turkey at Thanksgiving, her honey-glazed and sugar-crusted ham at Christmas, and the big pot of spaghetti she would make for us kids. I will never forget her Christmas cake, with Santa and the reindeer nestled in a snowy scene on top. It was almost too pretty to eat. It didn't occur to me until I was older that we were Jewish and it might be a bit odd that we were celebrating the birth of Jesus.

Grandma Margaret taught me how to cook and take pride in my kitchen. My mother hated the kitchen and hated to cook, and as I stated before, her meals were nothing to write home about. Grandma was an "Emily Post" graduate who kept a nice, orderly home. My mother's house felt like a zoo. Mom used to say she felt neglected as a child because grandma was off being a socialite and was rarely at home. But I doubt that was the cause of all her problems. Grandma died when I was only 22, so our time together was short. But I cherish the time that I did have her in my life.

WILLA

Willa and her husband Bob were members of my grandmother's house staff. She had worked as a housekeeper for some well-known celebrities but believed that gossiping was unkind and uncouth, and thus never talked about them. When my grandmother moved to a smaller house, she had less need for Willa's help. Since my mother was a completely incompetent housekeeper, Willa came to work for us as well. She was a truly amazing, refined African American woman from the South, who was trim, fit and ageless. No one ever actually knew how old she was, as she would never discuss her age. She and Bob owned a little house in South Central Los Angeles.

Willa and her husband never had any children, for reasons I never knew. She would take the bus to our house or Bob would drop her off. Willa would enter our home, dressed beautifully in a tailored dress, coordinating sweater, and sometimes a hat. She and my grandmother were alike in so many ways, they could have almost been sisters. They both had an unflappable demeanor and dressed elegantly. Willa showed up every day, always right on time. She would come in, go into the bathroom and change into her starched white zip-up dress and white shoes. Willa spent the day at our house, cooking, cleaning, doing laundry, and ironing. She was a surrogate grandmother to me. She taught me about housekeeping, cooking, and attempted to teach me how to be a "proper" lady (well, at least she tried). She would also stay with my brother and me whenever my parents traveled.

Two days a week Willa would cook dinner as part of her duties, usually on the nights my mother would work. Thank goodness! She'd make extra so we'd have leftovers to get us through a few more meals. Willa also taught me about pride, being proud of yourself regardless of who you are or where you come from. She emphasized living by certain principles. Willa was one of the most consistent, well-adjusted figures in our household. She would come during the week, arriving in the morning after I had already left for school. I always could depend on her to be there when I got home. I don't think she ever missed a day except when her husband had a stroke and soon after died. Willa was strict, but in a compassionate way. She was one of the only adults in my life who set limits and followed through.

Of all the people in my life, Willa was probably the only one who understood what I was going through with my mother. She knew my mother was mentally ill, but demanded I respect her anyway. "She's still your mother," she would say. She reassured me by adding, "I know, I know, things aren't always easy. They will get better. Just believe in yourself." Willa knew that, one day, it would be important for me to understand what my mother was going through, and that she couldn't help herself. Willa was stable and didn't get flustered. She was very grounded and helped ground me. She helped me feel more secure in my crazy, chaotic home environment. In her white dress, she looked like an angel. She was an angel to me. Willa also taught me about not giving up, which has come in handy a multitude of times in my life.

MARGE

Marge and Ed were our next-door neighbors. They were a married couple at least 10 to 15 years older than my parents, and were already living in their home when my mother and father moved into their house. When I was three years old, I sat on the top bunk of my bunk bed and stared out the window that overlooked Marge's driveway and backyard. I liked to watch Marge garden. One day she saw my little face staring in her direction, smiled and waved at me. When I was around five we became friendly and I started going over to her house after school to visit with her. She was known in the neighborhood as "the candy lady" because she had an insatiable sweet tooth and loved to share her treats with the kids on our block. Shortly after Marge and I began our afternoon visits, my dental check-ups became less than stellar. Mom blamed my cavities on Marge. She told Marge if she did not limit my candy consumption I would not be allowed to visit her anymore.

Marge, who had never been able to have children of her own, took me under her wing. She was affectionate and literally taught me how to hug. I remember the day like it was yesterday. I was ten years old and my father had just had a heart attack. I was staying with Marge while my mother was at the hospital with my father. Assuming I needed some comforting, Marge approached me to give me a hug. She wrapped her arms around me, but I just stood there limply, with my arms at my side. Realizing I was not responding, Marge gently said, "Wrap your arms around me and squeeze. Now that's how you give a hug." She was also a great cook and shared her culinary skills with me. Marge was a good influence who helped me gain some much needed self-esteem. We also filled a void for each other.

Marge was a homemaker, and everything about her resonated nurturing wife and mother. She did all her own cleaning and cooking. She was devoted to her husband. She was in good shape and took daily walks down the hill where she lived. Her husband Ed would pick her up at the bottom of the hill and they'd go out for dinner. Like Grandma Margaret and Willa, Marge never wore pants. She took pride in her appearance. She was slim, dressed stylishly, loved jewelry, purses, and gloves, and her hair was always looked perfectly styled. She was so different from my mother, who was obsessed with her appearance but too consumed by anxiety, depression, and an eating disorder to put herself together. Also, like the other two influential women in my life, Marge loved to cook. I remember going over to her house after school, right around the time she was making dinner. She taught me how to prepare a meal and called me her "official taster." She especially loved to bake, which I enjoyed too.

My relationship with Marge was about baking, cooking, and bonding. I soon realized she was someone I could talk to about anything. She noticed that I was extremely shy and uncomfortable with myself. I was a little girl who thought she was overweight, which was probably influenced by my mother's own food and body issues. In addition, my mother had chopped off my thick curly hair into a pixie cut, because she didn't have the patience to care for it. I thought I looked more like a boy than a girl. In those days, the fashion was for girls to have long straight hair, and they would even iron their hair to make it straight. My skin was milky white, which some people told me was beautiful, but I thought I looked like a ghost. I had green eyes, which I received compliments for, but at that time blue was the popular color so I saw that as yet another flaw. I couldn't imagine how anyone would want to be my friend and was terrified to approach anyone for fear of rejection. Marge helped me overcome that. She helped me appreciate my inner and outer beauty, and taught me how to talk to people with comfort and ease.

We would role-play scenarios. Marge would pretend she was a little girl I didn't know who wanted to meet me. She'd say, "Hi! I'm Cindy. What's your name?" I'd reply, "Hi. My name is Peggy." Marge taught me how to be more confident in social situations. She told me that people would come over to meet me because they were interested in me. She reassured me that they would be scared as well. "They just want to have a friend too," she emphasized. I rehearsed with her. I learned how to be more confident and comfortable talking to people by observing her people skills. She taught me that if I was authentic and sincere, people would like me. It was unusual that someone would spend that much time with me and offer me so much encouragement and support.

Marge wanted to make my difficult home life a little easier. She and Ed would take me to interesting new places and teach me new things. We did a lot of unique activities together. When I was about ten years old they took me to a classic car show held on a golf course. At that time I was just starting to grow out my thick curly hair. So here I was an already awkward child, who looked more like a boy than a girl. I have ivory-white skin, which most people told me was beautiful. But I felt like a ghost. I had green eyes that I was told were beautiful, but I didn't believe it. I wasn't interested in cars at that age, but I was happy to be anywhere with them. We approached a vintage Rolls Royce and peeked inside. A boy my age dressed in a suit and tie was sitting in the back seat, looking bored. Marge said, "Well hello!" in her usual warm and inviting voice. The boy looked at me and said, "Hi! Want to come in?" Marge gave me an assuring nod, so I opened the door and got in. This was an opportunity for me to practice my new people skills. I climbed in and visited with the boy until it was time to go. That was the first time I was in the backseat of a car with a boy. At least that one time it was a classy car!

Marge helped me begin to believe in myself and feel more comfortable being me. At the end of the day, after one of our outings, Marge would send me home with something that belonged to her, something that she wanted me to have, to keep us connected in body and spirit. She treated me like a daughter. When Marge met me, she saw how badly I needed a mother figure in my life. Wherever we went, she would tell people I was her daughter. She lit up when I was with her.

I had an amazing relationship with Marge for many years and always appreciated how much she loved me. The summer before fifth grade, I came home from three weeks of sleep-away camp and saw a "For Sale" sign on her front lawn. I was in shock. I ran to her house and banged on her front door. When she answered, I said, "Why didn't tell me you were moving? I thought you would never leave me." She saw the tears in my eyes and replied, "We would never intentionally leave you. I wanted to tell you myself before you saw the sign. But it has become impossible for us to live next door to our other neighbors. Their son has vandalized our house numerous times, and we can't stay here anymore." I was broken hearted. I thought Marge would be next door to me forever, providing me everyday with the stability, the support, and the love I lacked at home.

Thankfully Marge did not entirely disappear from my life. She made a point of staying in touch with me. She and Ed would pick me up on Sunday afternoons and take me on outings. When we were together it seemed as if nothing had changed. This continued until I was old enough to drive myself, and then I would go up to her house in Bel Air for dinners. We remained close for many years.

4

THE GOOD DAUGHTER

— (1974–1985) —

I wasn't the only one who was affected by being raised in our household. My brother David was as well. While I became shy, unsure of myself and self-destructive, he coped with the chaos in our family by focusing on becoming a very successful businessman and filling emotional gaps with big boy toys and collectibles. I was in high school when David left to attend college in northern California. Even though he hadn't always been a source of support, I felt somewhat abandoned by him. Living at home with Joan became increasingly more difficult after he left.

I was envious of my brother's ability to come and go as he pleased, leaving me without a buffer between my mother and myself. The conflict between my mother and myself increased. There were a lot of arguments. I resented David's ability to compartmentalize and ignore the sense of obligation I felt to take care of our parents. David would tell me that I could leave town as well if I wanted to. But I believed if I moved far away, the family would fall apart. I took on the role of the "good daughter" and became the fixer and the healer in the family. Fulfilling this role has been the ultimate challenge of my life and that is probably why I eventually became a therapist.

It was so unpleasant with just my mother and me at home most of the time. I shouldered all the craziness and became what we call in psychology the "identified patient" in the household. The identified patient tends to be a child in the family who acts out due to conflict between the parents or because of perceived pressure to keep family secrets. They become the squeaky wheel who can function to bring estranged parents closer together by forcing them to focus on the troubled child, or who force the family to finally face and deal with their secrets.

Occasionally I got the opportunity to housesit for friends and that was the only time I had any peace. The chore of taking care of my mother was emotionally overwhelming. The burden increased with my brother gone and dad aging. Dad's motto was, "Don't upset your mother." But I couldn't take it anymore and started rebelling at age 13. I grew my hair out to my waist. I didn't care that it was curly and wild, which was in style in my crowd, "the last of the flower children." Dressed in hip-hugger bell-bottom jeans and halter-tops, I acted out by breaking curfew and experimenting with drugs.

Even though there were some consequences for my rebellious behavior, they were never consistent and certainly did not stop me from continuing to act out. The harshest punishment I received was being grounded for a week after coming home late from visiting with friends. Apparently I wasn't very good at time management, because it seemed like I was always getting grounded. I remember when my friends would come over, and I would have to tell them I couldn't go out. They would say, "Again?" But being grounded didn't stop me from having a good time. My friends would hang out on the front lawn and talk to me through my bedroom window.

By this point my mother had started to suspect I was heading down the wrong path. This was probably the only insight she ever had about me that was true, perhaps more motivated by her concern for appearances than for my well-being. One day she searched my room for cigarettes, which I was indeed hiding, and found a letter hidden in my underwear drawer that gave details about the questionable activities I was involved in at that time. She found out I was ditching school with my friends to go out for lunch and hang out at the beach, and sneaking out my bedroom window at night to hang out with my girlfriends and high school boys. I had no sense if I was pretty but I sure was popular with the older boys. Could I have hidden the letter in a more obvious place? Was this the proverbial "cry for help?" Unable to cope with what she read, Joan rushed off and shared the letter with her psychiatrist. The psychiatrist suggested she get me some help.

True to form, rather than deal with it herself, and since my father was an old-school, uninvolved parent, my mother forced me to see my own therapist. This was my first experience with counseling. I was 15 years old. The therapist was Freudian and, true to that orientation, mostly listened, nodding her head and not saying much more than, "And how did that make you feel?" I doubt she said more than 30 words in the span of a year. The therapy didn't help me. We never discussed any issues that were truly important, such as living with a crazy mother and an absent father, and how this resulted in me having zero self-esteem.

It is now widely accepted that in most cases cognitive-behavioral therapy works better than psychoanalytic with children and adolescents, because this population generally needs a more practical approach to changing their behaviors. In this case, I was the identified patient sent off to therapy to be "fixed" in order to make life easier for my mother. But the reality was that I wasn't broken. It was the whole family system that needed repair. This is a common mistake that parents often make when they aren't willing to look at themselves and their own issues.

It wasn't just my home situation that was adding stress and pressure to my life, school also played a part. I had scored highly gifted on IQ tests and was enrolled in gifted programs. Up until high school I did well in my classes, but it always seemed like everyone else did better and didn't have to work as hard to achieve good grades. My inability to concentrate and focus made it very difficult for me to function academically. My organizational skills were horrible. I could never remember to bring all my textbooks and school supplies to class, and I couldn't seem to stop my mouth from moving a mile a minute. By the time I started high school, I just couldn't keep it together anymore. I lived in a constant state of confusion, with no clue as to what was going on in my classes. I felt like I was living a lie.

I was told I was intelligent, but school felt so difficult that I had a hard time believing it.

Rather than feeling like a failure because I couldn't keep up, I chose to be rebellious and covered up my humiliation by acting like I didn't care. I would often cut classes at school and hang out with friends at a nearby coffee shop, or go to someone's house or the beach and get high. I gravitated towards other kids who also hated school. At times I would attempt to return to school, but, because I had missed so much class time, I couldn't understand what we were studying and felt like I was in a bad dream. I finally got caught in the eleventh grade by the girls' dean. After noticing that I had been absent multiple consecutive days, she called my mom to inquire about my health. That was the last straw for my mom, first the letter, and now truancy. My mom gave me an ultimatum and said, "If you can't live by my rules, then maybe you shouldn't live here at all." In retrospect, I realize my mother probably said that out of frustration and anger. However, I took it literally and began planning my escape.

Soon after I got caught I was expelled and left home. I moved in with a high school friend who already had her own apartment in Santa Monica. I attended continuation school, worked at a day care center, and got a second job as a hostess at a restaurant. I would go to school until 12:30 p.m., and then take the bus to work. Continuation school was a good fit for me. I could work at my own pace and had a coach who provided me with one-on-one instruction. I finished high school early, before the semester was over. My grades improved dramatically. I graduated, got to walk with my class, and started attending community college.

After I left home I had limited contact with my parents. I would see them on occasional weekends and have lunch or dinner with them at the yacht club. It was best for me to meet with them at a neutral place. In fact, I think we got along better without me living at home. I could determine how long to stay. My father would get upset and ask, "Why can't you spend more time with us?" I didn't tell him that it was because I didn't want to be around my mom. Still, I did feel guilty. Dad wasn't there for me, but he hadn't necessarily hurt me either. I felt bad about him being alone with her, but it wasn't my responsibility to save him from her. He would never have left her because the guilt would have killed him. Even though I tried to distance myself from my family, over the years, I still did things for them out of guilt and a feeling of obligation. I couldn't just abandon them. I loved them, I just couldn't live with them.

I finished high school, started attending community college at night, and was working two or three jobs to pay my part of the rent. No matter how hard I worked it seemed like I was always broke. I didn't own a car because I couldn't afford the insurance. So I hitched rides with friends and with strangers, or took the bus. But I was happy to be free and didn't really care. I was still a teenager and marriage wasn't even remotely on my radar yet. I just sort of figured, "Maybe one day I'll meet someone, settle down and have children. But for now, I'll just keep doing what I'm doing." I frequented the under-21 nightclubs with my roommate and our friends. There were times I was lucky to have made it home in one piece. I hadn't yet learned how to set boundaries or have respect for myself as a woman, and was seeking love and attention indiscriminately. As a result, I put myself in some very unsavory and dangerous situations.

I continued this lifestyle for a couple of years. My roommate left to move in with her boyfriend. Another high school friend took her place. While working as a cashier at a local hardware store, I met a man I started dating. Shortly after, we moved in together and got engaged (What was I thinking?). We were both 19 years old. He was tall and handsome, and appeared to be responsible. He was also romantic, at least at first, and apparently liked me. It didn't take too long until my fiancé started showing his true colors. He was extremely jealous, controlling, and physically abusive. It was very confusing to me. Even though my parents were neglectful and my mother emotionally abusive, they taught me that physical violence was not acceptable. I knew I had no choice but to leave him.

I arranged to move out while he was at work one day and moved in with another girlfriend. After that, I had a series of empty relationships. I was lonely and wanted companionship. I dated a lot, went barhopping and dancing almost every night, and spent way too many evenings with strangers. My ex-fiancé met someone new, moved in with her and offered me our old apartment. I took it and that's where I lived on my own for the next nine years. During that time, I dated a lot but never really connected with any one man. I was hesitant to enter into any other serious relationships. Trust had become a huge issue for me, yet I continued to put myself in a variety of risky situations.

I was victimized over and over again, without realizing what was really going on. This is a huge issue with young women, especially those who come from dysfunctional backgrounds. They figure if they go out on a date and let a guy buy them dinner, they now owe them something in return. Personally, I had no concept of "red flags." When my kids were old enough, I made sure they were educated. I told them, "The minute the hair on the back of your neck stands up, get out of there. There are a lot of evil people in the world who will manipulate you and use you." No one had ever told me that. I had no idea that I could say "No."

5

TRICK OR TREAT

(1985-1990)

My father, who lived across the country from his relatives, idealized the concept of a close nuclear family that would always be there for one another. That was his expectation, but that wasn't the way it turned out for him. It was partly his fault. And of course my mother had her problems. How could my brother and I learn about healthy family relationships if he and mom weren't good role models? Nevertheless, he advised me to "think about the future." He said, "If you don't have a family, you'll be alone the rest of your life. Find someone to marry so you won't be alone. Find someone to have as a close friend, a companion, a source of security." I thought, "Sure dad, I guess that makes sense. Maybe one day I'll take your advice." The way my father put it sounded so practical that I couldn't help but wonder if he had ever actually loved my mother. Did he consider her a close friend, a companion, and a source of security?

When I hit my late 20s, the majority of my friends were marrying their longtime boyfriends. At that time, I recalled what my father had said and decided to start dating with the intention of getting married. That is if I could find a guy I liked enough. I secretly checked off a 20-question list with all of my dates: is he already married, is he a good provider, reasonably attractive, does he like his mother, does he drink excessively, does he already have children, does he vote, etc.? Last but not least, is he Jewish? Religion didn't really make a difference to me, but I remembered my father saying, "Life is hard enough as it is. When making life changing decisions, try and limit the number of obstacles you invite into your life."

After ten years of working multiple day and night jobs and attending classes two days a week, at 28 years old I earned an Associate Degree in Liberal Arts. I applied for transfer to a university to complete my bachelor's degree and was accepted at the University of California, Los Angeles. I received the notification within a week of meeting my future husband Izzy. My roommate and her friends, who were all members of a Jewish youth organization, introduced me to him. They were going to a Halloween party, a fundraiser for City of Hope, and invited me. I went along for the heck of it and that's where I met the man I wound up marrying.

I knew what was important to me in a man by this point in my life. Above all else was a sense of humor. When Izzy was introduced to me, he was dressed up as a proctologist! He held out his rubber-gloved hand to shake mine. I looked at him and said, "Really? I'm not touching that hand!" He started laughing. That was his love at first sight moment. The same night, I met another guy who was a sex therapist. He was dressed as Zorro, with a sword. Nothing Freudian there! I dated both men for a while, but Izzy won out. During our first date, he acted really goofy, which at first made me question his maturity. He sent me flowers the next day with a note thanking me for laughing at all his dumb jokes. It was that clever move that won me over, along with his beautiful blue eyes, dark wavy hair, and thick black mustache. I went through my proverbial checklist and he passed. I started to think Izzy might be "the one."

We lived in different areas of the city and had two separate apartments. He lived in Brentwood and I lived in West Hollywood. We decided if we moved in together we could save money. So after dating for six months, and with his mother's encouragement, Izzy moved in with me and we got engaged. I went to school, worked part-time and took care of our apartment. He was working and making headway in his chosen career as a television advertising executive.

I had lived alone for so many years, in my own apartment, that I had grown accustomed to my ways. I was used to having my own space, keeping things the way I wanted to keep them, and not having to share. I was a private and very independent person who wasn't used to having to consider someone else. It was really difficult for me to adjust to living with another person.

The situation was further complicated by the fact that Izzy's parents were Eastern European Holocaust survivors, which creates a unique culture in a family system. My family had been in this country for multiple generations. Izzy and his family immigrated to the United States from Israel when he was four years old. My mother-in-law was the sole survivor of her immediate family and my father-in-law spent ten years in a Siberian work camp mining coal. Along with those horrific experiences come a lot of unhealed wounds, which manifested through depression, anxiety, fear, and a bleak outlook on life. They were saddled with a lot of loss, fear of abandonment, and survivor's guilt. That had a huge effect on Izzy.

His family was very close and had difficulties with boundaries. It was also hard for them to envision a future beyond today. It was not in a happy, live in the moment kind of way. Holocaust survivors often lived with post-traumatic stress from their original fear of believing that the Nazis could storm their home at any moment. They could be suspicious and mistrustful of outsiders. I, on the other hand, was the eternal optimist, believing if you trust people and work hard you will get what you need in life. They never felt that way. My mother-in-law had lived a comfortable life in Europe, but then lost everything, including her family members, when she was only 12. After Izzy's family immigrated to the United States they settled in the Fairfax district of Los Angeles, a neighborhood with other European immigrants, and created their own little village. Many of them spoke the same language and shared the same customs. They had a quiet understanding of what they had all been through, and it was challenging for outsiders to comprehend.

My future husband's family clung tightly together, in a way that showed love and support, and was completely foreign to me. In the culture I grew up, parents launched their offspring as soon as possible. It was a sign of success to have your children out and on their own before they even hit their 20s. The rule of thumb in our house was, once we turned 18 years old, if we were not in school full-time, then we needed to be out on our own with a job. I guess this was my parents' way of showing me what the world would be like if I didn't have an education. Izzy's family was over-involved, always in each other's business, whereas in my family, there was too much privacy, secrecy, and disconnect. His family was more of an open book. They protected each other by bonding in a group. I was used to protecting myself by being alone and closed off.

I found myself immersed in this whole other culture that I did not feel a part of. In my family, I had been the youngest and had little experience being around small children. I had taken care of kids at my summer camp and day care jobs, but this was different. Izzy had a niece and a nephew, ages two and eight, and his sister would frequently stop by, unannounced, with them in tow. I grew up in a family where personal space was respected. If you were going to visit someone, you would always call first. Initially I had a hard time with their lack of boundaries, and they had a hard time with me being what they viewed as rigid.

They would stop in while I was cramming for my college exams. I felt like I was expected to drop everything and visit with them. I remember one time when my nephew showed up with chocolate smeared on his hands and face, and he proceeded to climb and then jump on my white couch. I cringed while my sister-in-law did nothing, as he left chocolate fingerprints on the furniture. Growing up, I had nothing that was really mine. Now I had my own apartment and my own furniture that I had worked hard to afford, and here was someone coming in my home, disrespecting my stuff, and letting their child stain my couch.

When I complained, the response I got was, "He's just a two-year-old, he doesn't know what he's doing."

When I told my husband later on, he looked at me like I was the world's biggest bitch. He and his family seemed to think that I didn't understand children, and that I was cold and standoffish. His sister told me that I was too particular. "When you have your own children, you'll need to have more patience and learn that there are some things you have to let go." I responded, "When my children are climbing on my white couch with chocolate hands, then that's *my* children." I think she got it.

I just grew up differently. I could not imagine letting a chocolate-smeared child out of the house, much less taking them to someone else's home and letting them jump on their furniture. I had to learn to assert myself for the first time in my life. Moreover, I realized that I wasn't just marrying this man, I was also marrying his family. It was tough in the beginning. They had no appreciation for my point of view, which triggered a lot of my old issues. As a result, I started to question my decision to marry into a family that was so different from mine.

One night, as we were both lying comfortably on the couch watching television, Izzy said, "Get me a beer." I looked up from my spot said, "Excuse me? Are your feet working?" He replied, with a puzzled look on his face, "Yeah?" I said, "Why don't you get your own beer from the fridge, and you can get me one also, please." Before Izzy and I met, he would go home every weekend to his mother's house and lay on the couch watching football. His three-year-old niece would bring him a salami sandwich and a beer on a tray, which his family thought was adorable. I realized with shock that this man was a prince. The way his family treated him and his sense of entitlement really rubbed me the wrong way. No one had ever waited on me.

If I was going to marry this man, he needed some reprogramming. I told him, "Look, if you want me to get you something, you are going to have to ask me politely. Then I might consider it. And if I get it, I expect a thank you." At first he never said "please" or "thank you." I told him it would really help if he would. He didn't think he needed to. He thought it was implied. I responded, "How are we going to teach our future kids to be polite, if we don't role model it for them?" I realized that this is probably how his mother had trained him. They would cater to him and he'd get whatever he wanted. He was never taught proper etiquette, whereas I grew up with an Emily Post "school of etiquette" graduate. I had to reverse this or we would never last. I taught Izzy to use the words "please" and "thank you." To me it was just simple appreciation, and luckily he caught on fast.

Izzy was also a practical joker and sometimes there was a sarcastic quality to his jokes. He didn't get that his jokes could be hurtful. I remember when his best friends met me, they told him, "You better keep this one because you may not get another chance with a girl like that." They were warning him not to blow it with me.

But Izzy definitely had his good qualities as well. He was a litle gruff on the outside but had a huge heart, a (mostly) wonderful sense of humor and could fix anything around the house. I noticed what a beautiful relationship he had with his niece and nephew, and felt confident that he would be a great father. Izzy was the kind of guy who would give the shirt off his back for someone in need. A friend who had known him for a long time told me that my husband-to-be had cared for his father when he was dying from stomach cancer. After that, he took care of his mother as her son and surrogate husband. A part of me admired this. It told me that he would be there for our future family. But, in the beginning, it was hard for me to understand the way in which this family functioned. I thought, "What grown man still allows his mother to buy his socks and underwear?" I told his mother that I'd be buying them now, or he'd buy them himself. I did however value that he was a family-oriented person. Every night on his way home from work he'd call his mom to find out how she was and say hello. I thought if a man loved his mother, he'd probably make a good husband and father. I just had to make sure there were a few boundaries.

Our families were from different sides of the track. I grew up comfortably middle class, with highly educated parents who had professional careers. He grew up the son of immigrants, with a father who barely learned English. The family spoke Yiddish at home. They were blue-collar people, with no formal education. His mom worked retail and his dad was a house painter. My husband and I saw the world in different ways, but at the end of the day our basic values about family, charity, and religion were the same, which has helped keep us together all these years.

I never felt that either of our upbringings were better than the other. They were just different. In many ways my husband helped me to appreciate family, and that the relationships we have with our family members are a lot more important than material goods. He learned a lot from me as well. He began to understand and appreciate personal space, and what it meant for me to feel safe and secure. I needed to feel in control of my own environment. The intrusive behavior, the lack of respect and consideration I initially felt from Izzy and his family triggered old feelings of being unsafe, neglected, and invalidated. To feel like this was happening all over again was hard to tolerate.

The difference in our families was also an issue for our parents. My mother thought because my future husband had attended temple with his father for the high holidays that they were Orthodox and therefore "too religious" for her. Ironically, it was my parents who attended temple more frequently, for the cultural and social aspects. In addition, my mother was a competitive person and probably thought I'd like my mother-in-law better than her, and that my husband's family would pull me away from her.

When I was finishing my courses at community college, and before I met Izzy, my father offered me a deal I couldn't refuse. "If you cut back on your work schedule, and attend school full-time so you can finally graduate with your AA degree, and continue on for your bachelor's degree, I will supplement your income and your mother will pay your tuition." I moved out of my apartment where I had lived alone for nine years into another apartment with a roommate so we could share household expenses.

Several months later, after graduating from Santa Monica Community College and while waiting to hear from the universities I had applied to, I met Izzy.

Coincidentally, my roommate was moving out to live with her fiancé, which meant I would need to find a new roommate. It was at this time that my future mother-in-law, Luba, suggested that we could save some money if her son and I moved in together. So we did. My mother decided that I was his problem now and instructed my father to cut off my rent support. Needless to say, Izzy wasn't pleased with her decision. But he loved me and wasn't going to leave because of my mother's selfish control issues. We managed to get by financially but this created resentment before we had even tied the knot, and it lasted for years.

When we were planning the wedding Joan refused to let Izzy's mother contibute in any way, because that would give Luba the right to have a say in the wedding planning. In my mother's mind, it was her wedding. We wanted a rock band. Joan disapproved and told us we had to pay for that ourselves. When the band was performing, she approached the band leader and asked if they could play show tunes instead of rock'n'roll. Luckily the band knew who was paying them and ignored her. My mother disapproved of the fact that Izzy's mother smoked. So she purchased "no smoking" signs and put them on either side of the stage. Luba wanted to add a few additional friends to the guest list. Joan thought she had enough friends coming already. I told my mom not to worry; they probably wouldn't be eating because they were kosher.

My mother was so inflexible and unyielding. I think she always thought people were trying to take advantage of her in some way. I later caught myself acting just like her, being uptight about my nephew with his chocolate hands on the couch and people popping in whenever they pleased and infringing on my personal time. I realized I had adopted some of my mother's characteristics, being stringent and inflexible, and decided that wasn't the way I wanted to be. It was a big adjustment, not only getting used to my husband's family but also having to share my life with another person, but one that ultimately changed me for the better and prepared me for eventual parenthood.

I had to learn to adapt and take things as they came. I was going to school full-time, working as a personal assistant to a psychotherapist, and taking care of my mother. After the first year of marriage we bought a house and I was taking care of that too. We were settling into life together and growing closer day by day. After graduating from UCLA in 1989 with a BA in psychology, I was hired full-time by a marketing firm. Two years later, with Izzy's career going well, we decided to start a family.

6

IT'S A GIRL!

—— (1990) ——

It was Thanksgiving morning of 1990. I woke up at midnight with pains in my stomach. I thought to myself, "Damn, shouldn't have eaten that chili for dinner." After making numerous trips to the bathroom and dealing with increasingly sharper pains, it occurred to me that I might be in labor. "Nah," I said to myself, "how could I be, I am still three weeks away from my due date?" Nevertheless, I woke my husband and informed him that the birth of our first child might be imminent. Without missing a beat, he reached for the 300-page natural childbirth book laying unopened on the bedside table, which I had asked him to read four months earlier. I watched him in disbelief and said, "Really? Like that's going to help us now!" At this point it was still only two in the morning, and because of my usual self-sacrificing, caretaking personality, I elected not to disturb the doctor until a little later.

We were expected for Thanksgiving dinner at the home of good friends who lived in Orange County. I figured by 7:00 a.m., with the pains gradually increasing, it might be a good plan to call and let our hosts know we would not be joining them. I called my girlfriend Cindy, who happened to be a pediatric nurse practitioner and had three children of her own, and explained my situation. Her response was, "Why the heck are you calling me and not your doctor?" I told her I did not want to disturb him so early on Thanksgiving morning. She laughed and said, "That's what you pay him for. Hang up and call him, now!" I stood up to get the telephone number, and at that exact moment it all began...my water broke. True to my nature, I chose to take a shower before heading off to the hospital so I wouldn't offend the doctor. I also figured that, because this was my first child, we had plenty of time before the baby would be born.

I was right. Twelve hours into labor the doctor determined that this little baby I was carrying was enjoying life in the safe comfort of my belly way too much and was in no hurry to come out. But the delivery clock was ticking. The doctor told me that once a woman's amniotic membrane breaks, the risk for infection to the baby increases, so the ideal delivery window is within 12 hours. In order to speed up delivery I was given an intravenous (IV) dose of a labor-inducing drug called Pitocin, and assigned to a delivery bed where I labored until the big moment arrived.

I had grown very close to my sister-in-law Sarah by that time and allowed her to join us in the delivery room just in case I needed a little more support. As I lay in bed hooked up to the IV and a baby heart monitor, Izzy and Sarah sat nearby playing gin rummy and eating turkey sandwiches from the hospital vending machine (the closest thing they could find to a Thanksgiving meal since the cafeteria was closed for the holiday). Every so often I had to remind them that I was in the middle of delivering a baby. I hollered, "Hey! I hate to interrupt your game, but I'm having a baby over here and could use a little help!"

The doctor would pop in every so often and check on me to see how far I had progressed. At one point he informed me he was running home to have dinner and the hospital would page him when I was close. I said, "Okay, but don't eat too much turkey and pie because I want you wide awake when the time comes."

At 8:59 p.m. our baby girl was born. I knew I was having a girl, but Izzy wanted to be surprised. Unfortunately, the surprise had been ruined because my very generous mother-in-law and sister-in-law had bought me a full supply of pink diapers but did a poor job hiding them in their living room. My husband kept teasing the doctor about how easy his job had seemed. He said, "I could have done that, gotten a baseball catcher's mitt and caught the baby when it popped out. It didn't look that hard." (Always the joker.) For me it was an amazing experience. It was hard to believe that a beautiful little child came out of my body. The doctor held the baby up and remarked, "No mistake here who the father is." He was right. All she needed was a mustache and she would have been her dad's twin. Even at birth Julia looked more male than female. In celebration of her birth, the hospital gave me a pink badge that said, "It's a Girl!" I still have that badge in a keepsake box next to my bed along with some old bracelets and toy license plates that bear her birth name.

Ever since I can remember I dreamed about having two children, one boy and one girl. I desperately wanted a girl so I could have that mother–daughter relationship I had been denied. I had fantasies of what that mother–daughter bond would look like. We'd get manicures, go to the beauty salon, talk about menstrual cycles, her dates, plan her wedding, and do whatever else I thought mothers and daughters are supposed to do together. I had all those things in mind that I never experienced with my mother. It was like a secret life I imagined in my head. I was determined to be the mom my adoptive mother Joan had been incapable of being. I was thrilled to find out my first child was a girl. I would finally have that female family connection I so desperately craved and the opportunity to be a good female role model for my daughter. But life had a different agenda in store for me.

I remember clearly the first night in the hospital, when the nurse brought the baby to me, after she'd been checked out and bathed. It took a while for it to sink in that I had just had a baby. That this was my flesh and blood. For the first time in my life, another living being had a direct genetic connection to me. I knew this was profound, but at the same time I was in shock and feeling somewhat numb, like I was an observer in my own life. I did not form an immediate bond with my daughter. In truth, I had no idea what to do. It was hard to trust that I could instinctively know the right things to do. After a couple of nights in the hospital, I was sent home with my new infant, Julia. I was completely unprepared for what came next. I was weighted down by guilt over not being able to connect. I started to have fears that I might be like my adoptive mother, unable to be a nurturing, caring, attentive parent. I felt protective of her and knew I would die for her, but I didn't really know how to love another human being from the depths of my soul.

A few days after Julia's birth she developed jaundice, which required her to spend several hours a day under special lights to help her little body excrete the excess bilirubin in her bloodstream. This added to the stress of being a new mom and made it even more difficult for me to adjust to early parenthood. Because my mother was useless as a parenting resource and I had no younger siblings to care for growing up, I had no clue what to do with a brand new baby.

Fortunately, I wasn't completely on my own. I had help from my mother-in-law and sister-in-law. They taught me how to care for a newborn. But it was still a very difficult time for me. Julia was colicky and a terrible sleeper. I would nurse her, she'd vomit then sleep for one and a half hours before waking and repeating the whole cycle again. She'd wake up hungry and crying. I was anemic and exhausted all the time. I felt agitated and then I would feel guilty for feeling agitated. In retrospect, I realize I had postpartum depression. When Izzy came home from work, I'd immediately hand her off to him. When he held Julia she'd calm down, but when I held her she sensed my anxiety and this limited my ability to console her.

Because Julia's jaundice had gone undetected for several days, the doctor felt it would be wise to run a blood test to make sure her liver had not been affected. Luckily there was no damage to her liver, but there was an elevated level of an enzyme in her blood that suggested there was something abnormal that would require monitoring for months. My husband and I would have to take Julia for monthly blood tests and she soon became traumatized by needles. Back then, I couldn't bear to see her in pain. The sound of her crying would trigger breast milk production and my milk-swollen breasts would ache, leak, and soak my blouse. Izzy was so worried about Julia's health that he insisted she sleep on his shoulder at night so he could keep an eye on her. As a result, she became attached to sleeping in our room for years.

Julia's elevated enzyme level never completely went away. When she was a year old Joan suddenly remembered that I also had "some sort" of anomaly as a child that my pediatrician recommended she monitor. But of course my mother never followed through. I shared this information with Julia's pediatrician, who suggested that I have the same blood panel done for comparison. My results matched Julia's, confirming we had the same condition. This was the first sign of a true genetic connection between another human being and me. Of course, eye color, smile, or nose would have been a preferable genetic connection as opposed to a genetic mutation. But hey…I'll take whatever I can get.

7

THE FIRST
TWO YEARS

— (1990–1992) —

The first two years of marriage are referred to as "the honeymoon period." But the first two years of motherhood were not a honeymoon for me. After a couple of months Julia's colic stopped and parenting got a little bit easier. I felt more comfortable meeting her physical needs but was still struggling with bonding emotionally. The first two months of an infant's life are so important for bonding. Because I was given up at birth by my unwed teenaged mother and spent the first two months of my life in a cold, steel, sterile environment until I was adopted, I didn't have that opportunity. My daughter now had that opportunity and I tried to do my best, and at the same time, grieved for what I had been denied.

A pregnant, unwed teenager in the 1950s was a scandal. When my birth mother was five months pregnant, she was sent away to a home for unwed mothers called the Chandler House in Chicago, to live until the baby was born. Chandler House was affiliated with the Cradle Society, the adoption agency that had taken me in as a newborn and a couple months later placed me with my adoptive parents. After I became a parent, I developed a need to find my birth mother in order to gather medical information.

My first step was a trip to the adoption agency in Chicago, where I was given a tour of the facility. The agency had a full-scale model of what the nursery was like back in the late 1950s. It had white walls, steel bassinets, and glass bottles. I was fed, clothed, and kept clean, and occasionally held by the revolving-door nurses. Everything was cold, white, and sterile, supposedly to protect us from diseases they did not have vaccines for in those days. It wasn't an abusive or dangerous place; it just wasn't the most nurturing environment. Moreover, the school of thought back then was that if you coddled children or held them too much, they would become spoiled. Not only was I in an ice-cold bassinet, ripped away from the warmth of my birth mother's womb, I didn't have consistent, unconditional love right from the beginning. It wasn't until years later that I realized I had been suffering from abandonment issues and an attachment disorder.

The next stop on the tour was the nursery, which had gone through a number of renovations since the time I was there. The nursery was warm and inviting, with pink and blue decorations on the walls. There were wooden cribs or cradles for every baby, soft, pastel-colored bedding, and numerous rocking chairs. The agency had a crew of volunteer retired individuals who came in every day to hold the babies. They rocked them, held them, and fed them on a daily basis until they were adopted.

The most poignant room I was taken to during the tour was the "Union Room." In the 1950s, adoption was "closed," meaning neither the birth mother nor the adoptive family knew the identity of one another. Therefore, the baby might never know their birth parent unless a search ensued. The "Union Room" was the room where the baby was passed to its new parents through a ritual whereby the infant was placed in a white wicker cradle then relinquished to their new family. A social worker would place the baby in the cradle and leave the room just long enough for the adoptive parents to enter from a different door and find their new child waiting for them. They would pick up their baby and embrace it for the first time.

I walked over to the white wicker cradle and thought, "That's so pretty." I reached out and touched it. The moment I touched it, I had this shooting sensation in my fingers that traveled through my arm and into my heart. Tears came into my eyes. It was at this moment that the social worker told me the story of the cradle and how it was at least 50 years old, and said that I had probably been placed in that exact cradle waiting to meet my adoptive parents.

This was such an amazing, surreal experience for me, to make the connection to my infant self having been in this place. Touching the cradle and feeling that energy fill my heart and soul was a wonderful gift, because in that moment I truly understood how fortunate I was to have my own children. I realized how much I did love my family and how connected I actually was to them.

What I learned from this experience is that, when children only get the basics in life and are deprived of the most important elements of parenting, it can cause serious emotional injury. It is so important that infants receive adequate mirroring from their primary caretakers. They need to have reflected back to them that they are the priority and the most important thing in their caretaker's world. Children need to know that they matter and deserve their parents' attention, affection, and unconditional love.

My hope was to one day have an amazing connection with my own children and meet all their needs. But with my first child I couldn't at first. We both had all these issues. Julia had a traumatic infanthood. I felt inadequate and unable to take care of her. I felt I was letting her down like my mother had let me down, not being able to do all those things I thought I "should" be doing. That was the hardest thing for me, the secret pain that I went through. I started to think, "What the hell have I done? Maybe I shouldn't be a mother. I don't know how to be a mother. Maybe I'm no better than my mother was." Izzy was good with the baby, but that also made me feel horrible. I was jealous that he could calm her down and I couldn't. That was supposed to be my main job, and I felt I was both failing as a mother and letting my husband down too.

Nevertheless, there was a silver lining. Because I wasn't able to be as nurturing for my baby as I had hoped I could be, my husband stepped in willingly and took up the slack. This allowed him to have an experience many fathers never have. It forced him to be a true hands-on parent and brought him closer to his daughter.

I was fortunate to have Luba and Sarah helping out, but it also felt intrusive. I wasn't used to all the attention. Not only that, but because I was feeling uneasy about how I was adjusting to being a parent, their willingness to help and teach me was a double-edged sword. I was thankful they were there for me, but the more they taught me the more I realized how much I didn't know and the more inadequate and frustrated I felt. Plus, accepting help from anyone has always been hard for me. It took a long time for me to accept that there are people in this world who actually enjoy doing things for other people, just because of who they are.

As time went on I started to see reflections of myself in Julia. She was an early talker and hasn't stopped since, which is a lot like me. We both have a lot to say, whether anyone wants to hear it or not. She loved music, music videos, and books from an early age. She loved to dance and sing. I saw more genetic connections as Julia grew older. Like me, she was an observer. When we would go to a social event Julia would take her time getting involved. She would sit off to the side until the event was almost over. In her little mind she was trying to figure it out, assessing and analyzing. Finally, after she had scoped out the scene, she would want to be part of it and join in. Unfortunately, by that time it was usually time to go home. This was exactly how I acted at social gatherings as a child. I had also been shy and socially phobic.

Julia and I were similar in that we both had giving and caring natures. She was considerate and always stood up for the underdog. She would befriend the kid in her class who was different or who had a problem. Julia was, and still is, a humanitarian, with an open, generous heart. When Julia was 15 months, I became pregnant again, all part of my white picket fence fantasy, with the two kids, one girl and one boy.

8

AND THEN THERE WERE TWO

——— (1992) ———

I found out I was pregnant with a boy and was thrilled. The pregnancy went well. Jay came three weeks early, just like Julia. I had a repeat scene in the delivery room, with my husband and my sister-in-law present. They gave me Pitocin again, and oxygen, because I was having trouble breathing. After the epidural, the doctor was paged. I felt pressure and a seven-pound Jay popped right out. He came out blue and the nurse rushed him away. It turned out he was bruised from banging against my pelvic bone. He also had jaundice, just like Julia. We had to put another baby in a glass box, under the light, not unlike the 40-gallon aquarium our bearded dragon lizard had lived in. Jay could only come out to be fed, changed, and given a quick hug or two. This time around, because I'd already experienced it once, it was a little easier, except for the fact that my father was in the process of dying from cancer.

When Luba came to the hospital to meet Jay, she took a good look and remarked, "Hmmm, who does he look like?" This time around it wasn't as obvious. She turned to Izzy and said, "Well, let's see. He's so fair. He could look like your uncle." Dumbfounded, I said, "He probably looks like my father." My mother-in-law responded, "How could that be? You're adopted!" I reminded her that I did have a biological father out there somewhere, and I had information from the adoption agency that he was blonde, blue-eyed, and fair-skinned. In retrospect, I realized she thought I was referring to Joe, my adoptive father, who obviously had no biological relation to Jay. In that moment it sounded to me as if she was suggesting I had no birth father, and that I was an alien and was hatched from an egg. Coincidentally, Joe was fair, had blue eyes and white hair by that time. So there was a slight resemblance. Despite his illness, he was able to come to the hospital to meet Jay. I have a beautiful picture of him holding the new baby.

I had two kids in diapers and it felt like I had twins. Julia was good with her baby brother and enjoyed holding him. She was as helpful as a two-year-old could be, fetching diapers for me, or picking up a burp cloth if I dropped it. But then I remember one time when I was sitting on the couch nursing Jay and Julia walked over with a mischievous glint in her eye. I had a sixth sense that she was up to something. I looked at her and said, "Julia, be nice now. Give the baby a kiss." She leaned over and gave him a gentle kiss on his forehead, then smacked his head and ran away. She turned around and looked at me with an impish smile from across the room.

Overall Julia was very good with her little brother. She was only home for a few months with the baby and me before starting nursery school. During that time,

I enjoyed meeting other moms and their babies, but that wasn't enough mental stimulation for me. There's only so much time I could spend walking around the mall, talking with other new moms about strollers, pediatricians, sleep patterns, and what pre-school our four-month-old will be attending in three years. So I started a bookkeeping business to help maintain my sanity and hired part-time domestic help. I realized it was hard for me to be alone with a toddler and an infant 24/7. Unexpectedly, this gave me a glimpse into how my mother must have felt raising two children close in age. I was fearful that I might be more like her than I wanted to be, but also felt a new-found compassion for what my mother had gone through, stressed by the responsibility of motherhood and not having the coping mechanisms she needed as a result of her mental instability.

I'd see the kids during the day but I had help so I could get my bookkeeping work done. This helped relieve some of the pressure and also enabled me to enjoy the kids more. I looked forward to seeing them, when Julia got home from pre-school and Jay got home from the park with his nanny. For me, this was a necessity. I realized the fundamental difference between my parenting and my mother's parenting was that I had a true desire to be a good mother. When I was with my children I was truly connected emotionally and bonded with them, something my mother was never able to do. I held no judgment over women who chose to be full-time moms, but it just didn't work for me.

My father's health had declined to such a degree that we had to put him in a convalescent home. I would try to visit my dad every evening, if Izzy was home or I had a babysitter. Mom would tell me, "You don't need to come today if it's too much." She had some understanding that I had my hands full. I understood that this was a difficult time for my mother as she faced the inevitable. She was about to lose her spouse of 40 years. Therefore, I made efforts to keep her life running smoothly, doing her bookkeeping and other chores.

It was a sad time for all of us. Here I had this new baby boy, and everyone was excited. My brother's son had been born a few months before Jay, so there were actually two new babies to celebrate. But I had to divide my time between my kids, dad, and providing emotional support to my mom. I had to balance welcoming a new life and saying goodbye to another. It's interesting, because as Jay developed, I saw similarities between him and my father. I was also thankful that dad had the opportunity to connect with Julia, his first grandchild.

I was exhausted, with a newborn, a toddler, and my business. There were a lot of emotions, and a lot of ups and downs. The kids were not good sleepers. Jay wouldn't nap and Julia didn't sleep well at night. Thank goodness she potty-trained herself at two years old. Luba would take the kids sometimes so I could visit my father. As time went on, my father's condition got worse. When my dad was on his deathbed, hours away from dying from prostate cancer, and in his last lucid moment before slipping into a coma, he made me promise that I would take care of mom. He said, "I can't let go until I know you'll take care of her." I dutifully told him I would. Two hours later, I left his bedside to make the burial arrangements, yet another thing my mother couldn't handle herself. I made a series of calls, looking for a mortuary, contacting the rabbi, and arranging the funeral. As soon as I finished making all of the arrangements and had hung up the telephone, the nurse came to inform me that he had died.

To this day I believe that my father had consciously held on until I had left his room. In fact, it's not uncommon for the dying to wait until their family leaves the room so the family member's last memory is not of the dying person taking their last breath. Jay was just three months old when my adoptive father Joe died. This left me with not only an infant and a toddler, but also my dependent mother, who was less mature than Julia at that time.

9

DANCING TO A DIFFERENT BEAT

—— (1993–2000) ——

During the pre-school years, I started to notice that my children's gender expression was not congruent with their biological gender. They played with the toys that would be considered typical of the other's gender. Julia had an affinity towards blocks. She liked to build things and play with trucks in the dirt and the mud. She received Barbie dolls as presents, but never showed interest in them. She also resisted any "girly" clothes. At that time Julia had thick dark wavy hair, like mine, that fell just below her shoulders. I couldn't put a headband on her to save my life. She would rip them right off. I tried to style her hair, but the most she would let me do was put it in a ponytail. Julia would tolerate a dress, but insisted on wearing shorts underneath them. Her favorite attire was pants or shorts and crewneck tee-shirts, and her favorite color was blue. My little girl wouldn't go anywhere without daddy's baseball cap on her head, turned backwards.

Julia enjoyed being read to, and preferred books about animals to fairy tales. She also loved watching musicals, especially *Mary Poppins*, and loved to dance and sing. She always insisted on being the male character when singing songs and acting out characters from her favorite movies or stories. Julia identified the most with Burt, the chimney sweep from *Mary Poppins*. At age three she received a toy drum as a present and chose to play with that over any of her girlie things. We had no idea at that time what an important role drums would come to play in Julia's life.

Jay was adorable with his long blonde curly hair. He enjoyed playing with Julia's Barbie dolls, imagining them as female action heroes who saved the male dolls from disasters. One evening when Jay was about five years old, he and his dad were watching a television show that featured young men and women in skimpy bathing suits. Jay said to his father, "When I watch the people in bathing suits, my penis feels funny." At first Izzy, being a hetero-normative guy, thought this was a sign of his son's attraction to females. He assumed Jay was responding to the girls in bikinis, not the men in Speedos. When he reported this to me, I said, "Oh? Did you ask him whether he was looking at the boys or the girls?" My husband responded, "Uh, no. I didn't think of that." He missed a prime opportunity to clarify his son's sexual orientation. Not that it mattered, but we were curious.

Jay felt very comfortable hanging out with Julia and her female friends. He would allow them to dress him up in his sister's clothes and put makeup on him. He loved the attention. It wasn't that Jay wanted to be a girl. He just wasn't into rough-and-tumble boys' games and sports, and simply felt more comfortable with his sister and her friends. I believe he identified more with their softness, which was ironic, because Julia wanted nothing to do with being feminine.

When Jay was around five years old, my husband started to become curious about whether Jay was gay. He felt the need for some answers so we sought out a child therapist. I was not concerned, but supported my husband in his search for clarity. The therapist we met with tried to put a positive spin on the situation. He said that Jay imagined female dolls as superheroes because he viewed his mom as a strong role model, and tried to impress on us how wonderful that was. I was flattered, but also pretty sure that the therapist was skirting the real issue.

In elementary school, Julia was smart and had friends. She embraced everyone, even the underdogs and outcasts who didn't have friends and had issues. Julia was openhearted, kind, and non-judgmental. I think she embraced the outsiders because she felt different inside and was drawn to others like her. Still, she appeared happy and active. She continued to enjoy books, music, and Broadway musicals. She liked to spend time with me and seemed well adjusted, except for the fact that she had sleep issues. Julia never wanted to be alone at night. She had a hard time being alone with herself. It was scary. Perhaps when she was alone in the dark, that was when she was most in touch with how different she felt, how uncomfortable she was in her own skin. Years later she confirmed to me that she did indeed hate being alone with herself and her thoughts at night.

When Julia graduated fifth grade, she was required to wear a dress. Our compromise was that she would wear a "skort" (a pair of shorts with a skirt flap in front) with a blouse and a jacket. She let me put her hair, which by this time was quite long, into a ponytail. I told her she could go to school with tennis shoes, but when it was time for the ceremony, she needed to put her sandals on. She said she would, and I believed she was mature enough to follow through. But later, as I watched the ceremony, I saw that my daughter was still wearing her tennis shoes. I thought, "Oh that little stinker!" She had planned this all along. I had to smile. I knew there were differences with my daughter, but I also knew that deep down she was a good kid.

During Jay's elementary school years, he was cute, smart, and got good grades. But he was shy, not terribly social, and had a hard time making friends. Jay was creative and liked to draw. Both kids had their IQs tested and scored in the gifted range. They were put in gifted classes. They were both high scholastic achievers, loved by their teachers, and graduated from elementary school with honors. Jay was in Boy Scouts and Julia in Girl Scouts. I was an active Girl Scout mom and noticed that when the girls in her troop wanted to play house, Julia always volunteered to be the husband. Yet she seemed to always have crushes on boys. She gravitated towards boys more than girls, which I didn't understand until much later.

Julia was social, active, and impulsive. I didn't realize until later that she was trying so hard to feel comfortable in her own body. She would dress tomboyish and act like a male. She got along with girls but her best friends were boys. She liked sports and played T-ball on a co-ed team. Jay played too but hated it. Team sports made Jay anxious and it was probably around this time that his OCD was starting to build. Julia liked T-ball but got too old for it. She was upset that she couldn't join Little League baseball, which was only for boys at that time. She did not want to play softball with the girls.

I thought it was important for my children to have some interests outside of school. It didn't look like sports was going to work out and anyway I couldn't imagine myself as a soccer mom. So I focused on their other strengths and interests, and realized that both enjoyed music. Julia wanted to play the drums. I agreed to let her take lessons when she was ten, if she would also take piano lessons. Julia took classical piano lessons for two years, along with drum lessons. Later on she learned how to play guitar as well, but drums were always her first love. Jay played violin in the elementary school orchestra, and continued to take lessons until he went to college.

It became obvious to me that what my children enjoyed was more art related than sports related. Jay took drawing lessons and showed some real talent. He was also into science and everything cerebral. He was deep in his own thoughts, an eccentric genius. I sent him to science camp one year, which he enjoyed. Julia was enthusiastic about taking acting lessons. Jay eventually found out that what he really liked to do was to write, while Julia discovered that performing and music were always number one.

Overall there were not a lot of big traumas during the elementary school years. Izzy was a little concerned about our children's atypical behaviors, more so for Jay than Julia. I felt it was okay for them to be whoever they turned out to be. If you want to push your children to be anything else, you are creating a sense of false self and that is a road to disaster. You're telling your children from a young age that it's not okay to be who they truly are. So I let my kids do what they were drawn to do, explore whatever interests they had, and play with whatever toys they wanted to play with. I was very open-minded and my husband attempted to be the same. Our children's differences did bother him more than it bothered me, which caused some conflicts between us down the line.

I started feeling restless and unfulfilled in my career. With the children now older and easier for Izzy to handle, I started to contemplate the idea of going to graduate school.

10

WE CAN GET THROUGH THIS

—— (1998–2001) ——

When Jay was seven and Julia was nine, I decided to fulfill my dream of continuing my education and becoming a psychotherapist. This was quite an endeavor. All through my school career I had been told I was smart, but academics were always extremely difficult for me. I had no idea why and always felt like I was living a lie. I was supposed to be smart and was expected to excel, but that wasn't my reality. So I faked it the best I could.

Later in my life, I felt driven to help people with similar afflictions (even though I was still unsure exactly what they were) so they wouldn't have to suffer the way I had. It's not uncommon for people who have had challenging lives to pursue careers in mental health. They call us "wounded healers," which definitely describes me. Becoming a therapist was the only way I could think of to be of service so I bit the bullet, applied, and got into a graduate counseling program. Izzy hoped that getting an advanced degree would also improve our finances and was very supportive. I went to a graduate school that had a minimum classroom commitment but a lot of studying. Izzy would take the kids on the weekends so I could do my work.

Overall graduate school was a positive experience. But, as usual, functioning in an academic environment was difficult for me. I completed all the coursework and did well, much to my surprise. I guess it was because I was really interested in the subject matter. When I was about to start working on my Master's thesis, which I was dreading, I finally realized why school had always been so hard for me. While attending a workshop on adoption, the presenter mentioned that there's a correlation between children who were adopted and attention deficit hyperactivity disorder (ADHD). A light bulb went off in my head. I said to myself, "Oh my god, I bet that's what I have."

I read the book *Women with Attention Deficit Disorder* by Sari Solden,[1] answered her checklist of ADHD symptoms (I got 19 out of 20), and then consulted with a psychiatrist. I received a positive diagnosis of a pretty serious case of ADHD and was prescribed medication that changed my life. It helped me get through the process of writing my thesis. I also hired an ADHD coach, who kept me on task. It was significant that I had asked someone for help, which has never been easy for me. My therapist at the time explained that I needed to line up a variety of resources to get me through, and I listened. During the process of learning about

---

1   Solden, S. (1995) *Women with Attention Deficit Disorder: Embracing Disorganization at Home and in the Work Place.* Nevada City, CA: Underwood Books.

my ADHD, I found out that there is a strong genetic connection. In other words, it runs in families.

When my children started having their own struggles in school, I reflected back and realized how familiar their experiences felt to me. School was very challenging for me from an early age due to my undiagnosed ADHD, which contributed to feelings of being different and defective. In the 1960s, the diagnosis of ADHD was fairly new, and mainly given to boys, because the symptoms manifested more as disruptive behavior such as calling out in class and not sitting still. No one really knew about the other manifestation of the diagnosis, the one more often displayed by girls. Those symptoms are inattention, inability to focus, and disorganization, which lead to daydreaming, as opposed to acting out behaviors. The symptoms are often more passive for girls, and the part that could be considered hyperactive is excessive talking. Back then, if girls were exhibiting what we now recognize as ADHD symptoms, their behavior was rationalized as simply not being good students, not interested in academics, and more suited for a domestic lifestyle. Thank goodness we've evolved from there!

School was torture for me. In elementary school, I had a teacher who used to talk about my "spring-loaded desk." I was constantly getting in trouble for my cluttered, messy desk. No matter how hard I tried to organize it, I just wasn't able to. I would also get in trouble for talking in class. In addition, I sucked my thumb until I was 12. That was the only way I knew to soothe myself. My second grade teacher called me out for sucking my thumb while we were resting our heads on our desks during "quiet time" on a rainy day and gave me a "D" in health. Being shamed in front of the class mortified me, and that was one more thing to make me feel crappy about myself. In middle school I replaced that habit with smoking cigarettes. I smoked until I was 21 years old.

In third grade we were administered IQ tests. I tested in the gifted range and was put onto an advanced academic track. Up until high school I did well in my classes, but never as well as others in the gifted program. It always seemed like everyone else did better and that it wasn't as hard for my classmates to get good grades. It was very difficult for me to read, almost impossible to stay focused on one paragraph at a time. I would have to read a paragraph over and over to comprehend what I had just read; this was an exhausting process. Thus it was almost impossible for me to keep up with my homework. What took another student an hour took me half a day. No matter how hard I tried, I never felt successful. I would ask myself, "How is it possible that I could be so intelligent yet feel so stupid?" By the time I started high school, I just couldn't keep it together anymore. I was supposed to be smart, but school felt like such an uphill battle.

When my son Jay was in fifth grade, he started to have behavioral problems. He would yell out in class. Moreover, he was impatient, couldn't sit still and was having a hard time concentrating. When I asked Jay what was going on, he told me, "I can't pay attention unless I'm doodling." Evidently that kept him focused. I had a conference with the teacher, who agreed to make certain accommodations for him. Jay was allowed to doodle during class. He was also allowed to squat in his chair, which helped him sit still. Per my suggestion, the teacher agreed that he could sit in the back of the class, so he wouldn't distract the other students.

It was clear that Jay, like me, had ADHD. With the genetic connection of ADHD now firmly in my field of knowledge, I had him tested by a psychologist and he was officially diagnosed. I modeled advocacy by making sure my son had the accommodations he needed to be successful at school. With the modifications he thrived and graduated from elementary school with a presidential academic award. This experience inspired the topic for my Master's thesis, which was a design for the reorganization of the public school education system. I felt strongly that children learn in different ways, and need to be taught in the ways that work best for them.

At the same time, Julia had started middle school and was having more and more trouble staying organized. Her backpack was a mess, which reminded me of my spring-loaded desk. She'd leave books at school and often forgot her homework. She would get frustrated and angry with her teachers. She talked a lot in class, in a disruptive way. She couldn't keep her focus for very long and her grades started to drop. My good little girl was melting down. I watched with a pained heart as my daughter grew increasingly frustrated, confused, and anxious.

When all this started happening with Julia, I took the same steps I had taken with Jay. Again, I wanted a diagnosis so I could advocate for her in the school system. In order to arrange for any of the special programs they offered, the school needed a formal diagnosis. I could have gone through the school district to get it, but there was a long waiting list for getting children tested. I didn't want my kids to fall through the cracks like I had so I took her to a psychologist and paid out-of-pocket a second time.

I was relieved to find out that my children had ADHD and not something else that could not be managed. After getting the formal diagnoses, I knew the appropriate steps I needed to take to get them the help that they needed, help that I never had at their age. I put together a treatment team to work with them. I didn't think they had been properly taught how to study or stay organized in school. A friend referred me to an educational therapist to work with the kids on their organizational skills and study habits. I consulted with a psychiatrist about possible medication and worked with their teachers on making accommodations.

I became Julia's taskmaster, helping her with homework and making sure she brought it to school. Jay, on the other hand, was obsessed with getting his schoolwork done. I would have to tell him to go out and play with friends, but he couldn't. It later became apparent that this was OCD, which he had in addition to ADHD. Jay's brain would overload and you could practically see the smoke coming out of his ears. He was so driven.

I accepted that I was going to have to focus more of my energy on my children's academic success. Eventually the combination of managing my own life and theirs was getting to be a little overwhelming. I made the decision not to work full-time and hired a college student to come over every afternoon and help them with their homework. Soon things started to turn around for both kids and they seemed to be thriving again. Little did I know that bigger storms were brewing just around the corner.

11

LIFE DERAILS

—— (2002) ——

Life was going smoothly. Julia, now 11 years old and Jay, now nine, were flourishing in school and I was moving forward in my new career as a mental health professional. It seemed as if we were back on track, until the night I got the phone call.

I'll never forget the voice on the other end of the phone telling me to sit down. "I have some horrible news to tell you," he said. I learned that my best friend Marci, the wife of my husband's closest friend, had died suddenly of a heart condition at the age of 46. Our children were close in age and had grown up together. They were like cousins, and she and I were like sisters. Her death hit me like a ton of bricks. I broke down and cried.

This was a devastating loss for all of us. In the minds of most children, only elderly people die. But now my children could no longer hold onto the illusion that parents are immortal and this affected them deeply. If Marci could die, then it was possible that I could die as well. They also saw me, their pillar of strength, in a moment of despair and emotional distress, which frightened them. Now they felt unsafe. If mom was in such bad shape, who would take care of them when they were in need? No longer was I my children's superhero, the "super-mom," the one who comforts them and tells them everything will be okay when they are scared. Now they saw me in my most vulnerable and emotional state.

This tragic event was only the beginning of a series of personal losses. First my best friend died, then my husband's stepfather passed away after a short battle with cancer, and soon after that my brother almost died from a dissected aorta. All of this happened within a three-year period. It seemed at the time that it was just one loss or trauma after another. Life suddenly seemed so fragile. My children started worrying about their parents' health and well-being. Anytime I got sick or felt slightly under the weather, they would ask, "Are you going to be okay, mommy?" Life had become unpredictable and they were scared.

In most cases children are prepared for death by losing a family pet before they lose a family member or friend. My children suffered the loss of one loved one after another. All of these events triggered a downward spiral for both kids. Jay was hit especially hard. Their feelings of insecurity brought on such shame, guilt, and sadness for me later on when I realized I hadn't been there for them in their hours of need. My parents expressed very little emotion when my grandparents died and never honored me when I had feelings about those losses. I had vowed that my kids would always feel protected, be allowed to have their feelings and express them. But I was in so much pain, and, because I had no real support, it was too difficult for me to give my children what I had been denied. During those years, I fell from the pedestal they had put me on and in retrospect, I feel like I let them down.

Jay's anxiety skyrocketed. He lived with the fear of something bad happening and his mother not being strong enough to take care of him. This may also have contributed to why Julia took so long to open up to me about her issues. My children now felt they had to take care of me. This was disheartening because it closely resembled what I had gone through with their grandmother. The whole dynamic of our family was changing in ways I never imagined, and I felt I had no control over what was happening.

Everything was uncertain and we were all feeling alone and sad. I simply wasn't able to focus on the kids and what was going on with them. I felt like life was going in slow motion. We were all in our own worlds, dealing with our grief in our own ways. Looking back now, it all seems like a blur. I graduated from my program and started working in my new field, as an intern at a counseling center. We were all just going through the motions of everyday life, not really connecting, not able to share our internal worlds. It was a very dark period for our family, but somehow we pushed forward.

12

I HOPE YOU'LL STILL LOVE ME AFTER I TELL YOU THIS...

(2002–2004)

Julia had started going through puberty when she was ten years old. She suffered from horrible cramps and migraine headaches. She matured early and was turning into a young woman. Julia was not comfortable with this process. She hated her changing body and insisted on wearing baggy boys' clothes to hide her increasingly feminine figure.

By age 12, Julia was doing well academically in middle school and had friends, most of them boys. Initially I assumed she was a tomboy because she enjoyed stereotypical boys' activities, such as riding bikes, playing basketball, and videogames. There were one or two boys she specifically liked to spend time with, and I naively believed she had crushes on them. So when she came into my room in the middle of the night and told me that a girl was harassing her at school because Julia had rejected her romantic advances, that made sense to me. The harassment continued and quickly escalated to death threats via the Internet.

Alarmed, I immediately consulted with the school guidance counselor, who informed me I had a criminal case. I went to the police and filed a report. I had saved copies of the instant messages with the death threats, enabling the police to trace them back to the girl. They paid her a visit at her house and told her to stop, but she denied she was the one sending the threats. However, directly following the police visit, the e-mails miraculously discontinued.

Shortly after that incident, the school guidance counselor called and told me that the *Dr. Phil* Show was doing a "Back to School" episode on cyber-bullying and asked if I would be interested in appearing on the show. I said yes and was featured on the show, along with the principal and the guidance counselor. I was the proactive mom who had advocated for her daughter and took action to protect her kid. That was my first media exposure.

A year after the *Dr. Phil* Show aired, Julia came into my room once again in the middle of the night to talk about something that was weighing heavily on her mind. She proceeded to say, "I hope you'll still love me after I tell you this. I think I like girls." I was not entirely surprised and responded, "Really? Glad you figured it out. I had my suspicions. Of course I will love you no matter what." I went on assuming she was indeed a lesbian. There were a couple of girls she seemed to be interested in. But, between the ages of 12 and 14, it became more and more apparent that this was not all that was going on with her.

At the same time, my mother had a bad fall and broke her hip. I was pulled back and forth between trying to figure out what was going on with Julia and attending to my mom. After a month-long struggle in the hospital, on her deathbed, my mother helped me heal from 46 years of hurt and resentment simply by saying, "I'm so sorry I wasn't a better mother. I hope you know I love you." For as long as I can remember, all I wanted was to hear my mother tell me she loved me. In that moment, I felt like I was standing in my daughter's shoes when she asked me if I would still love her as a lesbian. I finally felt seen and accepted by my mother, and it validated my commitment to help my children feel loved and accepted unconditionally.

At age 14, Julia's bubbly vivacious demeanor changed drastically. She became depressed, withdrawn, and started fabricating illnesses to avoid going to her new high school. At Julia's school, the demographic had a reputation for not being tolerant towards the LGBTQ community. Students like Julia were at risk if they were "out" regarding their sexual preference. Unbeknownst to me, Julia was being verbally and physically harassed at school because she dressed like a boy. She was afraid to go to school and started cutting class.

Concerned, we found Julia a therapist to help figure out what was going on with her. We assumed she was having adolescent sexual orientation issues. The counseling did not help. In fact, she got much worse and her situation at school escalated. She came home one day with a huge red welt on her forehead. I asked her what happened. She said, "Oh nothing. The dog scratched me." I looked at it and knew it was not a dog scratch. I asked again what happened, and she told me, "Somebody at school threw a soda can at my head."

I immediately called the school and made an appointment to talk to Julia's counselor. We had a discussion about her academic issues and, most of all, the bullying. The counselor tried to assure me that, although there were some rough elements in the student population, Julia would be protected. My instincts told me this wasn't true. As a long-time proponent of public school, I struggled with the thought of having to bail out of the system. But suddenly I was faced with a tough decision as to whether Julia could remain in public school. I knew I had to take action to ensure her well-being. But I felt a bit lost because I still had no idea what was really going on with her.

Julia's lack of attendance became a huge problem. Even though the school officials told me I could be held legally responsible for her truancy, I didn't feel I could continue to send my child to a school where I didn't feel confident she'd be alive at the end of the day. The counselor told me there was an alternative. They could recommend Julia for an independent study program, where she would meet with a teacher twice a week to get her assignments and take tests, and study at home. I looked into that and decided it was the best option for the moment. If she was homeschooled, I could then keep an eye on her and keep her out of harm's way. I removed Julia from the danger at school only to find out she was also a threat to herself. She entertained thoughts of ending her life and began acting out with suicidal gestures. By this time, I was a marriage and family therapist intern, and would leave for my job not knowing if Julia would be okay when I got home. So I started stopping by the house every few hours to check on her. In the safety of our home, she was able to concentrate on her studies and get through her classes. But she still didn't seem happy, and I knew there was something seriously wrong.

I sent her to a couple of different therapists, but her depression didn't improve. Julia became agoraphobic and wouldn't leave the house. The only thing that kept her going was her music. She attended a music school that she loved in Van Nuys called Join the Band® that teaches people of all ages how to sing and play musical instruments, and puts them together in groups to try out the experience of playing in a rock band. She also continued taking private drum lessons. Music brought Julia a lot of comfort during this difficult time.

Thankfully, because she was home and in a safe environment, Julia was able to begin the process of discovering what was really bothering her. I was still at a loss and worried sick. Julia was invited to go with her friends to see the movie *Hedwig and the Angry Inch*. It had become a cult hit similar to *The Rocky Horror Picture Show* with people joining what is called a "shadow cast" that is made up of actors who dress like their favorite characters, act out the scenes, and sing along with the songs while the movie plays in the background. The movie is about a transsexual punk rock girl from East Germany who tours the United States with her rock band as she tells her life story and follows the ex-boyfriend/band mate who stole her songs.

Julia loved the whole experience and went several more times before she joined the "shadow cast" of

Hedwig and the Angry Inch. A young transgender man, one of the actors in the shadow cast, befriended her. They really clicked and started communicating online. Through this friendship, it slowly became clear to Julia that her problem wasn't about her sexual orientation. It was about her gender identity.

Julia did research online and connected with an older transgender man who had just gone through the transition. He shared his experience and served as a mentor. It was all starting to come together for Julia. She had always felt more male than female. She searched computer chat rooms and found more transgender individuals to talk with. Now certain of her gender identity, she decided to confide in me.

I wasn't exactly sure at first how to wrap my head around this new development. In order to help me better understand, Julia printed out medical articles on the topic she found on the Internet. She emphatically told me that this is what she believed was going on with her. My first response was, "Are you sure?" It did kind of explain things. However, I was still a little confused about what it meant to be transgender. But I trusted that Julia was the best judge of who she was.

After confiding in me Julia seemed calmer and happier. I remember her saying, "You know mom, I thought I was a lesbian and liked girls. But that didn't entirely fit. So I continued to do my own research so you could understand what I think I am. Mom, I honestly think I'm transgender and meant to be a boy." It was starting to all make sense to me. I recalled when she was very young, around five years old, coming up to me and saying, "Mommy, I feel like I'm a boy inside. Yeah, I think I'm a boy." This latest revelation had no influence on how I felt about her. In fact, it gave me hope that now we could actually get her the help she needed to get back on track and moving forward with her life.

13

THE TRANSITION

———— (2004–2006) ————

I did my own research to get clear about what we were dealing with. I wanted to understand the process of transitioning. I realized we needed professional help. There weren't a lot of resources at that time. The only one who seemed perfectly clear was Julia herself. She was completely confident. She knew who she was now and insisted we had to figure out what to do so she could be the person she knew she was inside. It wasn't about sexual preference. She was transgender and wanted her brain to be congruent with her body.

I wanted to help Julia, but she was still fearful about telling her father. Afraid of being rejected, Julia asked me to keep all of this a secret from her dad until she felt comfortable telling him. She didn't think he would be as understanding as I was. Having no clue as to what was really going on, he thought that Julia's refusal to go to school and increasing isolation was due to her being rebellious and lazy. He had accepted the idea that she was a lesbian, but she didn't think he would accept this, which put me in a difficult situation. Eventually we had to tell him. He knew something was going on and wanted to know.

It turns out Julia was right. Izzy wasn't able to accept that his child was transgender and things got tense between us. He thought I was an irresponsible mother for entertaining this idea, and that Julia was just going through a phase. I repeatedly told Izzy, "This is real, not a phase." But he wouldn't listen. Izzy also thought I was largely responsible for Julia deciding she was transgender because I had let her go see *Hedwig and the Angry Inch* and hang out with "questionable people." The truth is, if I had not allowed her to see the film, she would probably be dead. Izzy was in denial and we fought a lot. It was rough on our marriage and on both kids. I tried to limit contact with him to avoid further conflict. My focus was mostly on moving Julia forward in her transition. Jay coped with the tension in the house by withdrawing.

Julia found a program for transgender teens at Children's Hospital of Los Angeles. It was called the Transgender Youth Risk Prevention Program and included a peer support group led by two social workers. The program was set up mostly for disenfranchised youths, who paid a low fee or could attend for free. It provided support, psycho-education, and medical treatment, including hormone replacement therapy (HRT). They were entitled to all of these services if they regularly attended counseling and peer support group meetings. From age 14 to 16, Julia attended the support group and also saw an individual therapist who was referred by Children's Hospital and specialized in gender identity issues. (See the Resource list at the end of the book to help find a program like this in other areas.)

I met other transgender kids in the program as I sat in the waiting room until the support group was finished. Julia wasn't old enough to drive. I talked to young people aged 17 to 22 going through the same thing as my daughter. Most of them were young men transitioning to become female. I realized what they had gone through, how difficult it had been for them, and this broke my heart. Most of the kids I spoke with had been thrown out of their family homes. They were living high-risk lives, doing drugs, prostituting themselves, and some had contracted HIV. Many had attempted suicide.

It disgusted and saddened me to hear about all of these parents who threw their children out onto the streets. Their religious orientation and/or their cultural or personal agendas influenced them to turn their backs on their children who needed them more than ever at this crucial time. I accept and love my children no matter what their sexual orientation or gender identity may be. Those parents may have been struggling with denial and guilt, feeling their child was a mistake, a problem, and defective. For those parents, out of sight, out of mind was the only solution.

I sat week after week in the clinic's waiting room, talking to the kids and listening to their stories. One boy told Julia, "You are so lucky. Your parents are supportive and you are not out on your own. I wish I had a mom like yours." It just would never cross my mind to abandon my child. I love and respect my kids, and I knew what it's like to be emotionally neglected as a kid.

Some people I confided in seemed to think this was easier for me because I was a therapist. I responded,

"Are you kidding? I'm a mother first." I couldn't help but be worried about her. It hurt me to see my child going through something so difficult, and I was frustrated that even though I was a therapist, I was lacking the knowledge and training to tackle this situation. However, one positive aspect of being a therapist was that I knew I couldn't do this alone because I was too emotionally involved. So, as I had done when my children were diagnosed with ADHD, I sought out resources and put a treatment team together.

Homeschooling allowed Julia the privacy and safety she needed to get comfortable with herself and to start the transition process. I got a call from Izzy, while I was out of town at a professional conference, that Julia took a pair of scissors and chopped off her long hair. That pained me. I had always loved her beautiful long waist-length hair, although deep inside I think I knew that she had grown it out to humor me. It was never what she truly wanted. Cutting it off was a strong statement on her part, it showed that she was ready to move into her new identity. She came out publicly as transgender, changed her name socially, but not legally, to Jacob (Jake for short) and requested that we start calling her by male pronouns.

Julia will now transition on these pages from female to male as she did in real life.

At first Jake let us call him "J.J.," a gender-neutral nickname, to help us get used to the transition process. The nickname was derived from Jacob, his new first name, and Joseph, which had been my father's name. He started binding his breasts. He was on the cusp of changing, looking more like a boy. But he still had a female voice. His dad refused to call him Jake or use a male pronoun. He was having an extremely difficult time letting go of his little girl. My husband was unable to accept Jake and support him in a positive way, and this hurt my son deeply. He had enough to deal with just working on himself. I didn't think it was right that he had to deal with his dad's disapproval as well. Because Izzy had been so close with Jake and his brother from the time they were first born, the rejection was devastating.

Izzy refused to get on board and at times put Jake in jeopardy by calling him female pronouns in public when he was trying so hard to present to the world as male. I felt unsupported. Izzy's behavior was detrimental to Jake's safety. He and Jake stopped talking. It was a constant uphill battle. Izzy acted out and was angry with me because he just couldn't understand. I believed in Jake's truth. I knew that to keep my child alive and help him develop into a happy, productive person, we were going to have to move forward with this whether his dad was on board or not. If this meant sacrificing my marriage to protect my children, then that was a choice I would have to make. I told my husband, "If you can't go with it, I'm leaving with the kids."

The tension was thick and we only spoke when necessary. Jay reacted to the conflict by withdrawing even more. The only reason I didn't leave my husband was ultimately for the sake of the children. Being a marriage counselor, I knew, if we got divorced, that the decision to allow Jake to transition or seek therapy had to be by mutual consent. But as a married couple, one parent can make that decision on their own. So I explained to Jake exactly what was going on, that he would have to deal with the turmoil in the house in order for him to be able to move forward with his transition. He understood.

Jake began HRT at age 15, getting testosterone injections while attending the program at Children's Hospital. Due to the fact that he was young his body responded well to the additional testosterone and his physical appearance changed quickly. Puberty was starting all over again but this time it was going in the right direction. His voice began to drop and he started to sprout facial hair and a lot more body hair. Jake was thrilled. The outside was starting to match the inside and he was becoming the person he always knew he was. The hormones helped to reduce his body dysphoria, his feeling that he was in the wrong body. But the one area that kept him from being completely content with his body was his chest.

Despite the changes, Jake was still depressed and a relatively high risk for suicide. Even though the excess testosterone made it hard for him to cry and express emotions, he was able to verbalize to me that he could never be truly happy about his physical appearance until he no longer had to hide his female breasts. In order to pass in public as a male he wore a compression vest to give the appearance of a flat chest. The vest was so tight that he could barely breathe. Jake would over-compensate for the compression on his chest by slouching, which caused back pain. Because his father was not on board, Jake worried that this was how he would have to live indefinitely. I assured him that

I would do whatever it took to make his life more tolerable, which included allowing him to have surgery without his father's approval.

After two months of hormone therapy and almost two years of individual and group therapy, we obtained the letters of recommendation needed for surgery from Jake's endocrinologist and his psychotherapist. Izzy reluctantly agreed to attend the consultation with the plastic surgeon. This surgeon was one of the pioneers of gender-affirming surgery and really knew his stuff. Jake was motivated to get this surgery done as soon as possible.

Izzy had a sudden change of heart the moment we entered the doctor's office. Jake walked in first and shook the doctor's hand. He took one look at Jake and said, "No question which way we're going, huh dude?" In that moment my husband finally got it. He started using the name "Jake" and calling our son "he." Now on board, Izzy asked how soon could we do the surgery. We were able to schedule it for the following January. To my relief, the relationship between Jake and his dad was now on the mend, and so was our marriage. Izzy and I were now on the same page and started working together as a team, which reduced the tension in the house and made life easier. Moreover, the moment Jake knew the surgery was scheduled he became a whole different person. I could finally breathe, or so I thought…

14

A DARKER TURN

————— (2006–2007) —————

Things were looking up for us until Jake was the victim of a transphobic-driven sexual assault. A young man aged 18, and two years older than Jake, who he had met through another friend, became fascinated and obsessed with him. This young man knew Jake was just beginning the physical transition to male. He started calling Jake and sending lascivious e-mails. He offered to show Jake what it was like to be with a "real man," to convince him to stay a girl. Jake called the guy back a couple of times and told this predator to leave him alone, that he was not interested. He blocked the young man from e-mailing him.

One night Jake went to the mall to see a movie. The friend he was supposed to meet didn't show so he left to go home. Jake walked back to his car, located on a side street to avoid paying a parking lot fee, unaware the guy was stalking him. Those were the days when kids were foolishly posting where they were going to be on social media. Jake had posted his destination on a popular social networking site. The guy, who was already stalking him on the Internet and on the phone, followed Jake back to his car, assaulted him in the front seat then ran away. Jake called me and told me what happened.

I told Jake to come right home and then immediately took him to the closest emergency room. We were instructed by hospital staff to call the police, and they directed us to a nearby rape crisis center where we were met by a social worker and police officers. It was a very long night. My sister-in-law joined us and it was comforting to have her there. They took Jake's statement and a doctor examined him. We went for a ride in the police cruiser to show the officers where the crime occurred. Then we went home.

Jake had clearly identified the culprit and the police had clear evidence to charge him, including DNA. The police knew exactly where to find him promptly and arrested him. There was something really off about this guy. He didn't seem to realize he had done anything wrong. A lot happened over the course of the next few days. A detective came over to our house to take another statement. We were contacted by the assistant district attorney and instructed to come down to the courthouse for a preliminary hearing. The guy pleaded out and was convicted of great bodily harm rather than sexual assault. I'm assuming his lawyer advised him to plead out and not go to court because the risk was too high that he would be convicted of rape and put on the list of sex offenders.

The perpetrator's sentence was 250 hours of community service, three years probation, and mandatory psychiatric treatment. His progress in therapy would have to be reported to the court. Also, he had to be enrolled in school and/or working full-time. In addition, a lifetime restraining order was put in place. It seemed like a small price to pay after the psychological and physical harm this creep had done to my child. I was beyond furious. This was a hate crime, and this monster had taken away my child's innocence.

The only reason we agreed to the plea bargain was to make this go away quickly so Jake didn't have to suffer any more trauma. Additionally, the defendant's parents had a slick defense attorney who tried to make it sound like the act was consensual and that Jake had wanted to have sex with a guy one last time as a female before completing his transition.

It was suggested by the prosecuting attorney that I write a letter to the judge before the trial started. The letter explained how much our family had already been through, and how this crime had put a damper on our healing process. The judge referenced the letter prior to sentencing. She was sympathetic and had seen us on the *Oprah* show, and acknowledged how much our family had struggled. The judge made the perpetrator stand and said, "I want you to understand the seriousness of what you did. I am giving you the maximum sentence allowed without jail time because this is your first offense. If you ever offend again, even a parking ticket, you will go to jail." I looked at the young man's mother and gave her a glare that said, "I hope you feel horrible. You raised this monster." I wanted her to see Jake and me, and to acknowledge the damage her son had done. At the same time, I felt sadness and compassion for how I imagined she must have been feeling, knowing that the little boy she had raised had grown into a despicable human being.

This whole incident was a nightmare. Just as Jake was beginning to feel comfortable with his body, he was violated. It made him more aware of what it felt like to be a vulnerable victimized woman, and reinforced his determination to transition. Now he knew for sure he had no regrets about moving forward with his decision.

I knew I was a good parent, and there was nothing I could have done to prevent this. But the incident brought up a lot of personal memories, feelings, and emotions that I had never allowed myself to feel when I had experienced being violated years ago. It reminded me of how I had not been protected by my own parents. When I was young I put myself in dangerous and abusive situations with men. I could definitely empathize with what Jake was going through. During the process of helping Jake work through this, I was finally able to begin the work I needed to do on my own past trauma.

At age 16 Jake had gender-affirming surgery (a bilateral mastectomy and chest reconstruction) and I nursed him through the painful recovery. He was happy with the results and not interested in going further with any other procedures. Penile construction surgeries like metoidioplasty and phalloplasty had not been perfected and were very expensive. But he wasn't interested anyway. As Jake always said, "It isn't having an actual penis that makes the man. It's about who you believe you are in your head and in your heart, not necessarily who you appear to be to the outside world."

Jake was learning to navigate the world as a young man. He started to gain an understanding of what male privilege meant. On the flip side, he was also learning how to live up to the chivalrous expectations our culture places on men. I've told my boys that when you open a door for someone, or give up your seat for the elderly, it isn't about chivalry; it's about being a good human. He also faced a number of new challenges, such as having to find men's restrooms that had stalls with doors, because he couldn't stand at the urinal. But Jake had no doubts he had made the right decision. To this day, if he regrets anything at all about transitioning, it's having to give up using the much cleaner women's restrooms. He was surprised to learn how messy men can be!

15

IN THE SPOTLIGHT

(2007)

The first media experience we had occurred after Jake had his chest reconstruction surgery. We received a call from a social worker with the Children's Hospital program who told us about an MSNBC documentary in the works on transgender young adults titled *Born in the Wrong Body*. The producer wanted a mix of transgender young people; a couple who had negative experiences and a couple who had positive experiences. In other words, transgender youths who got no support and were ostracized by their families, and youths who had supportive families. They wanted to compare their outcomes. They also wanted the project to have balance, and to show that there are some families that are dealing with this in a positive way and raising children who are well adjusted. We told the social worker we'd be interested and were given the number of the producer to call. That launched our media exposure.

The producer spoke with us and was intrigued by our story, a story of struggle but also one that was enlightening and inspiring. It was a different story, not a horrible negative one about parents who rejected their child and tossed them out on the street. MSNBC sent a producer, an assistant, and a film crew from New York to our home. They spent an entire weekend with us, following us around and filming us. They went to a Join the Band® rehearsal to watch Jake play. Jake was about to turn 16 and the producer even got into the car with Jake driving, taking her life in her hands, and drove around with him. We took her for cupcakes at our favorite cupcake store. She fell in love with them and later asked us to mail her some. We looked through picture albums of the family together. After they had finished interviewing me, Jake, and Jay, they went back to New York and edited the piece.

The result was an excellent documentary. It featured Jake and four other young transgender people in their 20s, trans-male and trans-female. They all told their stories. The documentary was informative, sensitive, and non-judgmental. The whole process was exciting for me. We didn't do it for notoriety, but because we felt it was important to share with the public how positive parenting and interaction within our family, and loving our children unconditionally, yielded a happy outcome. Even though there would be obstacles in Jake's life, he knew he had family and friends who loved him no matter what. Thus, his transition wasn't easy but it also wasn't catastrophic. If his circumstances had been different, he most likely would have killed himself. But he didn't. I like to think it was because of my dedication and my efforts. I was home with him. I made him call me and checked in on him throughout the day. I'd have my mother-in-law come over so he wouldn't be alone.

I decided to go public because I felt it was important to get my message across and to pave the way. My message to the world is that all families should be there for their kids. Whether it was our original plan to have our children or not, we chose to put them on this earth. Being a parent is a lifelong commitment. Therefore it is our responsibility to stand by our children and support them even if they choose to live their lives differently than we expected. We should celebrate their successes and get them help when we know they are struggling.

Being part of *Born in the Wrong Body* was a very positive experience. A year later, when Jake was 16 years old, we got a phone call from a producer for *The Oprah Winfrey Show*, who had seen the MSNBC documentary while researching material for a show on transgender youth. The transgender population was suddenly becoming a very popular media topic. Oprah's staff had tracked us down, along with one of the women featured in the original MSNBC documentary. They asked us if we were willing to be guests on her talk show. Coincidentally, this episode would be titled "Born in the Wrong Body," just like the MSNBC documentary. We agreed and two days later, they sent a crew out to LA to film us at home. It was starting to feel normal to have camera people around. Several days later, Jake and I flew to Chicago. Jay was not able to go. His first day at his new high school was the same day as the taping.

Jake and the transgender female were the two guests on the show. Oprah started by asking questions and soon she and the guests were having a lively discussion. I couldn't stop smiling. I was so proud of Jake. He handled the appearance like a pro. Mostly the conversation was positive, along with a couple of surprising moments. Oprah asked her guests a question (no longer deemed appropriate to ask) about how far they had progressed with their individual surgical transitions on their secondary sex characteristics (i.e., genitals and breasts). She asked the young woman if she had gone through any procedures yet. She replied that she hadn't had "bottom" surgery yet because she couldn't afford it. Then Oprah said, "I would imagine you would want to have your penis removed at some point since having a penis is the one characteristic that defines whether you are a man or a woman." With humorous defiance, Jake interrupted, saying, "Hello! Excuse me? No! Not necessarily!" Oprah realized what she just implied, that you couldn't be a man unless you have a penis, and was embarrassed. "Okay I stand corrected," she replied. She had inadvertently negated the reason Jake was on her show. In that moment Jake got across to America that gender identity is in the brain, not the body. Oprah and all of her viewers were educated about something that was of paramount importance to us.

During the commercial break, Oprah took questions from the audience. A discussion evolved regarding possible explanations for why the two guests were transgender. One audience member gave her opinion. She said to the guests, "I think you are just confused. God doesn't make mistakes. If you had a little more God in your life, you wouldn't be so confused." Jake replied, "Oh no, you have it wrong. I was confused, and now I'm not." I had tears in my eyes, along with many other audience members. In that moment they were feeling connected to Jake. Every parent in that audience would have loved to give my son a hug.

After the show they rushed us off to the airport and we flew directly home. Over the next couple of days, I went on *The Oprah Winfrey Show* website and read the comments people made about the show. As with every controversial subject, there are those who agree and those who don't. Those who didn't said some very cruel things. For instance, that I was an abomination for what I had done, and if only I could have found God everything would have been fine. One person said I must have been on drugs while raising my kids. Another questioned how I could have let my child go through hormone therapy and surgery at such an early age? My response was, "I'd rather have my child alive and happy than the alternative. Unless you walk in my shoes, don't pass judgment."

The latest research suggests that the earlier the individual begins transition, including hormones and surgery, the more successful the outcome. That is why there are proponents for using hormone blockers with younger children who exhibit signs that their gender identity may be in question. The reason for this is to slow down the puberty process and give them time to explore options. Once puberty begins, the process of transition is much more complicated. There were also quite a few positive comments on the blogs, about what a wonderful loving mother I was and how I did what was needed for my son. Others admired how strong, brave, and courageous Jake was.

The Oprah Winfrey Show experience went well. Our friends and family members were impressed. Strangers recognized us on the street and stopped us to tell us how much they appreciated the show. One Saturday night after the show aired we went to our family's favorite Italian restaurant for dinner. Our waiter came to our table and leaned over as he handed my husband our check. We had been a bit boisterous and I assumed he was going to tell us we were talking too loud. Instead he thanked us, in a whispering voice, for sharing our story. He said, "While we were setting up for dinner, we all saw you on *Oprah*. We were riveted and couldn't tear our eyes from the show. We recognized you and didn't get anything done for an hour. One of our staff came in late because he was watching at home. When he apologized for being late due to the show, we said 'no problem' and explained that we were watching it too." We were really touched to get this response. It was just what we had hoped to hear.

For a year or so after that, whenever we'd go to gatherings, there always seemed to be someone there who had seen us on *Oprah*. A client of mine came in a couple of days after the show aired. Before we started our session, she told me she had to say something. "While channel surfing about a year ago, I caught the MSNBC documentary. I never said anything because I didn't know if I should. I didn't want to put you on the spot. But then last week I saw you on *Oprah*. I figured now all bets are off. If you didn't want people to talk about it, you wouldn't be on the *Oprah* show." My client went on to tell me about parenting problems she was having with her three-year-old. "After I saw the documentary and the show, and learned about your approach to parenting, I knew you were the person

I wanted to see. I knew that no matter what issues I shared in our sessions, you would empathize and have compassion for me, and teach me to be a better parent." That was the affirmation I needed to know that the work we were doing was universally beneficial.

The decision to allow Jake to make the transition was difficult and one not made lightly, but I know I did the right thing. Our supporters on the blogs defended me against the negative and judgmental remarks. They praised us for sharing our story so that anyone experiencing the same thing would know they're not alone. They thanked us for blazing the trail. The bottom line is, whether they liked the decision I made or not, I had no choice. I had to make the right decision for my child and what was right for us.

Appearing on *Oprah* is what first turned me into an advocate. I realized how much work still needed to be done. I felt a calling to help parents who have children they don't understand and don't know how to help. I felt a desire to make the world better for Jake's community. At that time there weren't many of us, but today I'm one of hundreds of people who are doing this work.

16

THE RED CARPET

—————— (2008) ——————

The audience is clapping. I'm standing on stage behind Jake, who is at the microphone. We are at the nineteenth annual GLAAD (Gay & Lesbian Alliance Against Defamation) Media Awards in San Francisco, accepting an award for *The Oprah Winfrey Show* episode that featured us titled *Born in the Wrong Body*. The award is for outstanding TV show covering lesbian, gay, bisexual, and transgender, queer/questioning (LGBTQ) issues. GLAAD's agenda is to combat stereotypes and misinformation about the LGBTQ community in the media. This is their Academy Awards, and it's just as glitzy and star-studded as any awards show. They honor different forms of media, including film, television, and print.

We were invited in 2008 to attend the GLAAD Media Awards on behalf of Oprah Winfrey, who could not be there herself. Prior to the awards show we were ushered down a red carpet, with guests watching us and reporters interviewing us. I felt special. But what was really special was to be there because of my son's accomplishment. He sacrificed his privacy to make life easier for himself and others like him. He took a lot of risks. This was the validation he needed to prove to himself that what he was doing, with my help and support, was the right thing for him and for the whole LGBTQ community. It's the right thing for anybody who is different in any way, for anyone who does not conform to "the norm."

We walked from the red carpet into a pre-dinner VIP cocktail party. The guests included celebrities Judith Light, Billy Baldwin, Sharon Stone, Alan Cummings, and the mayor of San Francisco, Gavin Newsom. We met the editor of *The Advocate*, a publication geared toward the LGBTQ community. We were also introduced to the producers of the critically acclaimed film *Gods and Monsters*. I never imagined I'd be in a room full of so many influential people who shared the same mission I had for supporting the LGBTQ community and feel so welcomed. Everyone was dressed to the nines. We smiled, strutted our stuff, and faked being VIPs pretty well.

An hour later we were in a ballroom with at least 1000 people sitting at dinner tables, enjoying a surprisingly delicious meal. I was sipping a glass of wine and chatting up my neighbors on either side. Jake was a celebrity. Grown men were flirting with him and one invited him to come up to his room for an after-party. I gave that man the evil eye and said, "Excuse me? He'll get you 20 years in the state penitentiary, he's only 16!" Jake responded to the man's invitation in horror and said, "Eww…that's gross! I'm here with my mom!"

The well-dressed, middle-aged man sitting next to me at our table asked me who I was to Jake, and, before I could answer, he gave a creepy wink and complimented Jake on his taste in older women. Again Jake said,

"Eww…she's my mom!" I made friends with a group of women, all lesbians, who were also sitting at our table. Jake joked, "Lesbians love my mother." It felt good to be so accepted. Finally it was time for them to announce the award recipient in our category, "Outstanding Talk Show Episode." Even though Jake and I were hoping to win, we made an effort to play it cool and hide our extreme enthusiasm from the other guests and nominees at our table. We were thrilled when it was announced that *The Oprah Winfrey Show* won.

"Accepting for Oprah Winfrey is Jake and his mom Peggy." I turned to Jake to express my excitement, but he had already bolted from his seat and was running towards the stage. I half-ran, half-waddled to catch up, trying not to trip on my long skirt. Jake stood under the spotlights and grabbed the microphone. Everyone in the room was focused on him. It was suddenly so quiet you could hear a pin drop. In Jake's true fashion, he commanded the moment with total confidence. He knew exactly what to say and gave a beautiful spontaneous speech, advocating for the cause and thanking GLAAD for the award.

It was difficult for me to find words to express my excitement. I'm pretty sure I mumbled something. Oh well, at least one of us sounded intelligent. The audience clapped and we returned to our table. What a thrilling moment that was for both of us. I couldn't have been more proud of my son. I was enjoying being Jake's mom. But I was also aware of what a long struggle it had been for us to get here.

The whole evening was exhilarating. It was inspiring to see all those people there on behalf of the community.

It made us feel like we were not so alone in the world. It was fun to feel like a celebrity, but even better to see the impact our advocacy work was having on people and how much they appreciated it.

17

WHAT ABOUT HIM?

(2006–2008)

Jake was back on his feet and now also a media star. He had transitioned, was negotiating the world as a male, and was ready to re-enter school. I knew public school was not a safe place for him. Gender-neutral bathrooms were still a thing of the future, and very few public schools at that time had started staff sensitivity training regarding how to work with transgender students. I found out from another mother of a transgender child about a progressive private high school that had a strong non-discrimination policy. Jake applied and was accepted. He should have been entering his senior year of high school. However, he elected to repeat eleventh grade. With all he had been through, there had been some gaps in his education, and this would be an opportunity to fill them in.

Jay was far more advanced than the majority of his classmates, and needed to be intellectually stimulated. I sent him to a private college preparatory high school that was more suitable to his needs. It had been my hope that my sons would attend the same school. But I realized they did not have the same scholastic requirements and needed to be in different school environments. Jay was more academic and Jake leaned more towards the arts.

I had noticed when Jay was in pre-school that he had certain obsessive behaviors. He would become obsessive about certain toys and only play with that particular toy in a certain way. I believe Jay was born with the genetic predisposition for OCD. The beginning of his symptom manifestation started when Jay was eight years old, after the loss of my dear friend Marci. At that time the whole family was in crisis and both children became fearful of the idea that something bad could also happen to me. Jay's condition didn't really seem that serious at first. The symptoms seemed somewhat manageable and understandable due to the circumstances. He had been through a crisis and it made sense that he developed some post-traumatic stress disorder symptoms. I thought he would get through it and the symptoms would subside.

Over the next three years, we attempted to cope and heal from several large losses. It seemed like time flew by and before we knew it, we were back in crisis with Jake. I assumed Jay was doing fine. He was doing well in school, seemed to have friends, and there were no disciplinary issues. During the whole transition process, when Jay was about 15–16 years old, he became quiet and withdrawn. This should have been my wake-up call to pay attention to Jay. In retrospect, he hadn't been weathering everything we had been going through as well as I had hoped.

In middle school Jay was teased by peers for being overweight. He had an adolescent pot belly, the type of fullness many boys get before they hit their growth spurt and thin out. He also exhibited symptoms of a sensory processing disorder called "tactile defensiveness."

Jay was bothered by certain textures and also the tags in his shirts. We found an athletic shirt with no tags made of a fabric he liked. Jay also insisted on his shirts being three sizes too large. He would only wear that shirt with large elastic-waisted gym shorts. At that time, I thought the clothing issue was a symptom of his OCD. Between 13 and 14 years old, Jay became concerned about his weight.

We were all trying to be healthy at that time, eating better and exercising. Izzy let Jay go on a commercial weight loss program. It worked well for him at first and the pounds started melting off. Unfortunately, I didn't pay that much attention to Jay's dieting. I thought he was just trying to be healthy by exercising and losing weight. That's when his eating disorder symptoms, his fear of gaining weight and fear of fattening foods, started to manifest. Perhaps it was some attempt on his part to gain control over what seemed like an increasingly chaotic world.

Gradually Jay's health regime became an obsession. I noticed he was not really eating and was exercising for hours, several times a day. He started wearing baggy clothes like sweat pants and large sweaters, and became increasingly insecure about his body. He wouldn't wear shorts or a bathing suit, or go without a shirt. At that time, I was very distracted by Jake and wasn't paying attention to the signs. How could I have not seen what was really going on with him? My son felt like he had a constant tire of fat around him, what he called his "phantom fat." He knew intellectually that he wasn't overweight, but physically he felt like he was. He was always in an extreme state of high anxiety and depression. He went to school but was miserable and hated it. He believed he had no friends and that everyone thought he was weird. My son was a tortured soul. He was in a very dark place in his life. I could tell he was depressed, but didn't know how to pull him out of it.

Friends and family started to notice Jay was getting pretty thin and made comments. I recall Luba whispering to me, "He's so thin. Does he eat?" I didn't need to hear this from her. She would urge him, "Come on Jay, eat something." That didn't help. I was in denial at first, but when I finally started to face what was going on with him it tore me up. Jay, now age 16, was complaining about feeling light-headed and dizzy, and having weird sensations in his heart. He was irritable and fatigued all the time. There were a few days when I actually had to drive him to school because he didn't feel like he had the energy to drive himself.

When I finally realized there was something really serious going on with his health I took Jay to the doctor. The doctor weighed him then compared his weight to the year before. Jay had gone from 153 to 103 pounds. Moreover, his blood pressure and heart rate were extremely low. His heart rate was so low that it was causing him to pass out, get migraines and heart palpitations. His weight was dangerously low and he was really sick. The doctor informed me, "These are all the signs of anorexia nervosa. I believe that is what your son has." I replied, "Are you kidding?" My heart sank. I felt horrible that I, a therapist, had not recognized the symptoms. The doctor tried to console me by telling me that anorexia is less common in men than in women, and also that many parents do not see the signs until the disorder has become quite severe. "These patients go to great lengths to hide their condition. Their biggest fear is that someone will take the disorder away from them. The eating disorder is their best friend and how they cope with life."

The doctor told me Jay was on the edge of a danger zone, and close to needing hospitalization. I asked her, "What do you recommend we do?" She told me that eating disorders are best treated by a team of specialists. Jay's doctor helped us hook him up with a strong treatment team, consisting of a dietitian, a therapist, a psychiatrist, and a physical trainer to help him manage his body image issue. He started eating again and working out under the supervision of the trainer. The theory was that he would eat and gain, but the weight he gained would be turned into healthy lean muscle, so he wouldn't become overweight. Jay agreed to the plan. It took me a while to stop beating myself up, but, with the team in place, we started to see some improvements.

18

LOSS OF THE MANI-PEDI DREAM

———— (2008) ————

Although Jay's symptoms lessened, they were not completely eradicated. He had achieved some recovery, but was still struggling with obsessive thinking. The Minnesota Starvation Experiment (1944–1945) suggests that a malnourished brain is a breeding ground for obsessive thinking.[1] He would ruminate over and over in his head and couldn't stop the obsessive thoughts. Not being able to shut off his brain, especially at bedtime, left Jay exhausted all the time. He was obsessed with writing as well. During this period, he wrote a 90-page screenplay and sent out queries to thousands of literary agents. Jay's obsessive nature caused him to get hooked on an idea and not let go until he followed it through to conclusion. Even though this process was exhausting, I believe his brand of dedication, resilience, and endurance will be the driving forces that lead him to great success as a brilliant writer.

1   Tucker, T. (2006) *The Great Starvation Experiment.* New York: Free Press.

On top of everything else, Jay was also struggling with his sexual orientation. He had a hard time with relationships. Jay had a girlfriend for a short time, but she was mentally unstable and not healthy for him, so they broke up. He didn't date girls after that. When he was about 16 years old he met a young man online and they secretly started dating. I had questioned his sexual orientation when he was younger, but, when he had the girlfriend, I thought I might have been wrong and that he was straight. Then one day the truth came out.

Jay told me he was going to spend the day with a friend from middle school who was picking him up shortly. He got a text, said his friend was outside, and flew out the door. Jake overheard that Jay was meeting this particular friend and was confused, since he was coincidentally talking to that friend online at that very moment. Being the protective older brother, he asked the friend, "How can I be talking to you online at the same time you are picking up my brother?" The friend replied, "I'm not hanging with Jay today. What are you talking about?" Jay was busted.

I looked out the window and saw an unfamiliar car drive off. I called Jay and asked him, "Who just picked you up?" He told me again it was the same friend, unaware that Jake was currently online with him. I confronted Jay. "What are you actually doing and with whom? You lied to me. Come home now." Jay responded, "Well, it's a guy I just started seeing. I didn't want to tell you because I didn't want to hurt you. I know how much you went through with Jake. I wanted you to think at least one of your kids was 'normal.'" I said, "It's not your job to protect me. It's also not safe for you to be running around with people without me knowing who they are and where you are going. You should know I love you no matter what. Come home now. If this guy wants to keep seeing you, he needs to be introduced to me or you can't go out with him." Jay told me his new friend was shy. I said, "If you're worth it to him, he'll come in the house." From then on, Jay was above board and honest. He realized that his truth would not tear me apart. Not that it was a big surprise. Both Izzy and I had known in our hearts for some time that he was either bisexual or gay.

Jay went out with this young man for a while. The relationship didn't last because the guy wasn't "out" and his relationship with Jay had to be kept on the "down-low." They would go places but Jay couldn't hang out at his apartment or meet his friends. This didn't feel good to Jay so he ended the relationship. He grew tired of being a secret. Since that relationship, Jay has primarily dated young men. He has friends who are girls, but is only romantically interested in the same sex.

While I was going through everything with Jake, and all the attention was thrust on my oldest son, Jay was feeling invisible. I found out he was trying to protect me, even though I didn't protect him. This was a difficult thing to realize and deal with because I myself had been neglected and not protected by my own parents, and had vowed to always be there for my children. It pained me to realize that I had not been conscious of how Jay was being affected by the family crisis. I learned it's important to be aware that when one member of a family is in crisis, the whole family is in crisis.

I also wasn't aware that Jay was having trouble with Jake's issues and his transition. He felt like he had lost his sister. They were very close growing up. In fact, Jay's first word was "Yulia." He liked having an older sister. She was nurturing and mothering, and Jake still has that quality. They went to school together until high school. Jay's friends came over to the house and questioned what was going on with Jake. He didn't know how to deal with this, what to say about his sister becoming his brother. He felt even more like an outcast than he had before.

As soon as the transition started and Jake was getting all the attention, Jay became resentful. He was angry with Jake, me, and his dad. This threw a wedge into Jake and Jay's relationship. They would fight. I had to break up a fist fight more than once, had to physically pull them apart. I told them to talk it out if there was a conflict between them, not fight. Their conflicts could have been viewed as healthy sibling rivalry, the two of them finally separating and forming their own identities. It was also very male on male. They got really fed up and hostile with each other. Jake complained that he couldn't stand Jay's mood, that he was nasty and mean. Jay was depressed, withdrawn, and angry. Jake couldn't talk to him and didn't want to be around him. Jay hated every moment he was alive. Jake had moved past his darkness and couldn't remember how it had been for him. He forgot how depressed, nasty, and aggressive he was while struggling with his gender identity. Over time their relationship started to repair.

We went from being the parents of a caring older sister and an adoring younger brother to being the parents of two gay sons, and this was a whole different dynamic that affected everyone in the family. I felt a little outnumbered now that I was the only female, and was sad about losing my old mani-pedi dreams. But it wasn't like I had lost a child, my child was still there. I was mourning the loss of the opportunity to bond with a daughter, and realized my old hopes would never come to fruition. None of this changed my love for either of my boys. It had nothing to do with who they were as individual people. But the family dynamic changed nonetheless and there was a sense of loss for me.

But perhaps it was all a blessing in disguise. Because even though I am 100 percent comfortable with being feminine, I also have a strong masculine side. I realized that I myself wasn't really a particularly frilly type of woman. So, in the long run, having two boys feels more natural to me. I didn't have to go through a stage of competitiveness with a daughter, which is kind of a relief.

Still there were adjustments. I thought I'd be saving money by not buying beauty products and fancy girls' clothes. But then I was shocked at what car insurance cost for two adolescent boys. I have heard stories from my friends who have daughters that sometimes their favorite clothes and jewelry go missing. I never had to experience that (except on Halloween…). There were a lot more men's briefs in the laundry, a lot of socks and underwear to fold. After Izzy got through the initial shock and the struggles of the transition, he felt comfortable having two boys and related well to them. After a certain age men sometimes have a difficult time relating to a daughter, as they become young women.

Izzy didn't have to go through that. Neither of us had issues with our sons being gay and/or transgender, but, as parents who loved their children, we couldn't help being concerned for their futures. Being on the LGBTQ spectrum is becoming more acceptable, but it still adds another challenge to their life.

19

ON THE MEND

——— (2009) ———

In 2009, a couple of years after the first *Oprah* show, her people called us again and asked us to be on a follow-up show. They learned that Jake, now 18 and a freshman in college, was doing well. However, Jay, now aged 16 and a senior in high school, was not. The producers asked if both Jay and Jake would be willing to participate. I thought this could be an opportunity to share the important message that if one person in a family is in crisis, the whole family is also in crisis, and not to let any member slip through the cracks.

This show was a follow-up on where Jake was in his transition process and other aspects of his life, including his academic and his social life. Jake shared that he was now in a relationship, not with a woman but with a man, which really highlights that gender identity and sexual orientation are not related. He tried dating girls, but that never felt right. I suspect he was trying to fit into society's norm of being a male. He eventually realized that he was sexually oriented toward men. People asked, "Since he was born a female, why did he need to transition if he was going to be dating men anyway? Wouldn't it have just been easier to remain a girl?" Therein lies the proof that he knew in his head and his heart that his true gender was male. He needed to live his life as a male, which had nothing to do with his sexual preference. Jake identified as a gay male.

The show also explored how the relationship between the boys had become strained, as a result of Jake getting all the attention during his crisis and Jay feeling left out. Oprah talked with them about how Jay had developed an eating disorder, possibly triggered by a tremendous amount of personal loss and family chaos. Controlling his food intake and body fat helped give Jay a sense of internal mastery over his external environment. The boys had been very close, as they were only 23 months apart. They shared a bedroom, played together, and had mutual friends. It broke my heart to hear my boys talking about how they weren't as close as they used to be. But I felt hopeful in knowing this was a transition we were all going through and that at some point, because they had been so close before, they would one day be best friends again.

Following the taping of the show, Jay and Jake took a walk to the corner outside of the studio to take pictures of each other by the Harpo sign. It was cold and snowing in Chicago, so I wimped out and waited by the limousine. As a group of female audience members were leaving the studio they saw the boys, got excited, and asked if they could take a picture. Jake handed them his camera, thinking they were offering to take a picture of him and Jay. But what they wanted was to take pictures of themselves with Jake and Jay. "We love you guys!" they squealed. Women of all ages and ethnicities took pictures of themselves with the boys, making them feel like they were celebrities.

Later that day, while we were waiting in the lobby of our hotel for a limo to take us to the airport, four women from Texas who had been in the audience saw the boys and came over to talk to them. "The show was so great, so amazing!" they exclaimed. A bellboy asked Jake and Jay if they had also attended the show. The women exclaimed, "They were on the show! They were the stars!" Then they looked at me and said, "Mom, you are so lucky. You have such amazing sons. We saw the first *Oprah* show you were on and were hoping you would come back. We feel so fortunate to have been here for the follow-up show!"

The two appearances on *Oprah* launched our advocacy efforts. Jake's notoriety allowed us to start hitting the lecture circuit. First Jake and I were asked to give guest lectures a couple times a year at local colleges for their human sexuality and abnormal psychology classes. We also gave the first of several workshops at the Trans-Health Conference in Philadelphia. Then Jake and I started his foundation, Trans United with Family and Friends (TUFF), which he took over on his own once he became an adult. TUFF is a non-profit organization that raises money to give financial assistance towards transition costs for transgender and gender variant individuals.[1]

Because of his advocacy work and his good academics, Jake applied for a scholarship from the Point Foundation. They grant scholarships to students in the

---

1   www.tufforg.org

LGBTQ community. The application process is extensive and the awards are given based on the advocacy work the student has performed as well as their academic achievement. Four thousand students applied his year, 28 scholarships were offered, and one of them went to Jake. He received some financial assistance for college and, most importantly, was appointed a mentor who helped him develop his organization. Jake has a wonderful continuing relationship with his Point mentor who is a kind, compassionate, and loving man. He has helped Jake in many ways. Now that Jake is a Point Alumni and no longer his official mentee, I consider his mentor a part of our extended family.

What the exposure did for us, if nothing else, was give us some credibility. People say, "Oh, you were on *Oprah*!" It's given us a reputation for having something important to say. In truth, notoriety and fame is not going to come from 15 minutes on *Oprah*. The MSNBC documentary, on the other hand, is a piece of history. But there was a limit to how many viewers saw it. People watched *Oprah* because she's an icon and they trust her. They didn't necessarily tune in for a particular topic. So we were able to reach a more diverse audience.

One of the reasons we publicized our cause was to educate the ultra-conservative population who judge others based on their own personal, ethical beliefs. We wanted to show them that being transgender is not a choice, but a biological, medical reality. My children are unique, not freaks. In many ways, my family is probably more stable than many others. We live our authentic lives and are proud of living our truths.

The second time we were on her show, Oprah questioned Jay's comment about identifying as bisexual. He responded, "Well, actually, my mom taught us not to use labels. You love a person for their soul, not their gender." For the first time I realized my children actually listened to the things I say. My eyes welled up and I thought I was going to cry. I noticed two ladies sitting near me in the audience wiping away tears, and Oprah was also getting teary-eyed. Jay's claim to fame is that he made Oprah cry. I thought, "I guess I did an okay job after all." Both Jay and Jake handled being questioned on TV so naturally and so honestly. They did not shy away from discussing their personal struggles and baring their souls. Their goal was to try and help other people simply by sharing what they've been through. If they could get through this, then maybe someone who was challenged by similar issues would gain hope that they could too, and reach out for help.

20

LET'S TALK SHOP

—— (2005–Present Day) ——

I had developed a general private therapy practice where I was treating individuals, families, and couples, with my one specialization being adults who had attention deficit hyperactivity disorder (ADHD). After some time had passed and Jake was prospering, I was reminded of the young people I had met at Children's Hospital and how much help and support they needed. Since our family was no longer in crisis regarding this issue and I was not as emotionally affected by it, I decided to incorporate treating the LGBTQ population as a new specialty in my practice. I believe that we are where we are because that is where we are supposed to be, and, as the universe would have it, I received a telephone call from a local physician who had heard of me, inquiring whether I treated transgender individuals in my practice. I said, "Yes" and he referred a case to me. My new specialty took off from there.

There were no professional certifications for this specialty. So I continued to read up on the subject, do research, attend conferences and workshops, and talk to other professionals in this field until I felt truly competent to work with these clients. Some of the conferences I attended were the Philadelphia Trans Health Conference, Gender Spectrum, Gender Odyssey in Seattle, and the GEI Transgender Health Best Practice in Medical and Mental Health Care Conference. This really opened up my life. I traveled all over the country and met amazing people from all over the world. I started to promote my services. Through word of mouth and marketing, I got more referrals. Eventually, I had a nice balance of working with transgender individuals and other types of clients, which has continued until the present day.

This is a disenfranchised community that doesn't always have financial resources available for the help they need. I have compassion for this community as a result of my personal experiences with Jake. I feel fortunate that I am in a position to be able to offer them affordable therapy in order to evaluate if transitioning is appropriate for them and, if so, to help them through the transition process.

This is a more specialized field than many therapists are aware of, and requires specific clinical skills and understanding of what it truly means to be transgender. I have received negative feedback from clients regarding past experiences with therapists who claim to specialize in this area, but don't really understand the nuances of the transition process. They may in fact have had vast experience in the area of LGBQ, but don't realize that working with transgender clients requires more unique training and skills.

An important way to gain expertise is to have direct contact and compassion for the community itself. If you are a mental health professional who wants to go into this specialty, intern with someone who has experience, read books, go to conferences, and gather as much knowledge as you can. As with any of your clients, if you find yourself at a standstill or lacking information about how to proceed with a case, seek consultation from experienced peers. Additionally, there are now a lot more advocacy and health organizations in this field. It's crucial to get involved in those as well (see Resources at the end of the book).

Over the years, I've learned a lot about how to work with this community and their specific needs. I pride myself on being accepting and non-judgmental, and acknowledging that it's an evolving field and there will always be new developments and information to learn. My clients themselves have taught me a lot and have helped me to understand what it feels like to be transgender. It's about gender identity and has nothing to do with sexual orientation or preference.

It's important to know that gender exists on a spectrum.

In the United States, the gender spectrum was formed as an extension of the limiting gender binary that viewed man and woman as the only two gender options... It is a linear model, ranging from 100% man to 100% woman, with various states in-between. The gender continuum (sometimes referred to as the gender matrix) is an extension of this gender spectrum that includes additional gender identities... Viewing gender as a spectrum allows us to perceive the rich diversity of genders, from trans- and cisgender (identifying with or experiencing a gender the same as one's biological sex or that is affirmed by society) to genderqueer (denoting or relating to a person who does not subscribe to conventional gender conventions, but identifies with neither, both, or a combination of male and female genders) and agender (defined as someone who doesn't have a specific gender identity).[1]

Each of these clients is an individual, they each have their own process and there is no "one size fits all." Each person has their own story, their own experience, and transitions differently. The clinician must try not to project their own feelings, judgments, or agenda onto their client. There are different types of transitioning, social and medical. Some do one, some the other, some do both. That is determined by each person's individual situation. Some are unable to transition socially, medically, or both, even though they identify as transgender, because it could be detrimental to their career, their family relationships, and their intimate relationships. It could also be detrimental to their physical safety if they live in a state or country that does not protect transgender rights.

As a clinician, I follow the suggested recommended guidelines of the World Professional Association for Transgender Health (WPATH) when treating transgender clients (otherwise known as the "WPATH Standards of Care"). These standards have been proven to be good medical practice.[2] Besides following these

---

1   Source: Boundless (2016) "Gender as a Spectrum and Transgender Identities." *Boundless*, 26 May. Accessed on January 9, 2017 at www.boundless.com/psychology/textbooks/boundless-psychology-textbook/gender-and-sexuality-15/gender-414/gender-as-a-spectrum-and-transgender-identities-298-12833

2   If you are a clinician and interested in knowing more about the guidelines, go to the website: www.wpath.org

standards of care or assisting with transition, I follow a psychotherapeutic protocol as well. I start with a standard full mental health assessment, as I would with any new client. I assess for suicidal ideation, self-harm, depression, anxiety, mood disorders, eating disorders, substance abuse, physical, emotional, or sexual abuse, legal issues, relationship and other interpersonal issues.

The next step is to initiate a discussion about why they believe they are transgender. I take a full psychosocial history, looking for whether their story supports their belief about themselves. Other areas I look at are to what degree the client has gender dysphoria, defined as "the distress that may accompany the incongruence between one's experienced or expressed gender and one's assigned gender" (American Psychiatric Association, 2013). These feelings can be so intense that they interfere with the way these clients function in normal life. Do they feel disgust towards their genitals? Do they have a strong desire to be rid of their genitals and other sex traits? Do they feel certain that their true gender does not align with their body? Talking to a therapist is a valuable way to address the mental health issues that this diagnosis can cause. That is why I believe that psychotherapy is a crucial part of treating gender dysphoria.

I also try to determine whether other symptoms flagged in the general assessment were triggered by the gender dysphoria or are co-existing conditions. This may determine whether the client is stable enough to transition. It is important to address all possible mental health conditions because, even if the client does transition, that might not be the ultimate answer to their unhappiness. For instance, take the depressed middle-aged woman who thinks a facelift will change her life by making her look younger, but then has the procedure and is still unhappy because her core issues were not entirely related to her physical appearance. Changing the outside does not always repair the inside.

It is important for the client to know that "with every gain there is a loss, and with every loss there is a gain." After transitioning, they may finally be living in a body that is more acceptable to them. But they aren't always cognizant of what lies ahead and the new challenges they will be presented with. Ongoing therapy can be helpful as they continue to adjust to their new way of life.

The therapy isn't always just with the client, it often involves their support system. In fact, it's important to include their support system if the client chooses to do so. The whole family becomes the unit of treatment. As I said before, it's not just the transgender individual who is transitioning; the family is transitioning as well.

In the case of younger clients, it's usually their parents who come in first, sometimes referred by their pediatrician. The parents present with their personal concerns that their children appear to be gender-non-conforming and possibly transgender. The parents are often upset and seeking guidance. They want to know if I believe this is real, or just a phase. I give them resources and ask them to do their own research. I educate them about what it means to be transgender or somewhere on the gender spectrum. I explain that it's biological, not a choice. Because they love their child, my hope is they will figure out a way to accept them and support them through the process.

The adult client usually comes in on their own, in the beginning stages of exploring their gender identity. If they are in an established relationship, the therapeutic unit often includes the partner, if desired by the client. Often the partner needs to seek their own separate treatment if they are having a particularly difficult time adjusting. It can be a very challenging and painful situation for both the gender-non-conforming person and their partner. The partner starts the relationship with a person expressing as one gender, and that is the gender they are attracted to. When the person begins the physical transition, the sexual attraction may be lost. This puts a huge strain on the relationship. The transitioning individual is still the same person they were before, and it's heartbreaking for them when the partner they love rejects them. It's hard on the partner too. Often the partner feels like they have been betrayed and that the transgender person has been lying to them all this time.

Sometimes the partner feels guilty and wishes they were still attracted. The partner might think, "I should love this person simply because of who they are, but it's not that easy, sexual attraction is still very important to me." The guilt can lead to feelings of depression. In these cases, the relationship may end, or the partners may remain close friends but go separate ways romantically.

One of the most healing experiences in therapy is when the family members realize that this was not a deliberate deception. The transgender individual was unable to communicate because they were in the process of questioning their own gender identity.

21

YOU JUST HAVE TO LAUGH

— (2008–2014) —

Somewhere around the end of middle school and the beginning of high school, our house became the hang-out house for our boys and their friends. Young people knew they wouldn't be judged in our home. They would find an open ear and good food. We used to have a lot of kids come over all the time. This led to some funny situations. Friends of Jake's would come over as he was starting the transition. Some would be transgender males and others transgender females. I'd joke with my husband, "This is probably the only house where the boys pee sitting down and the girls pee standing up!" We'd shake our heads and say, "Only at our house!"

Pre-transition, when Jake was Julia and living as a lesbian, our house became the crash pad for tired teenagers after a night out. We had one rule in our home, very different from most other homes. The norm would be to have the boys segregated from the girls, in order to keep mischief at bay. But in our house, if Jake had a girl over and Jay had a boy over, the girl would sleep in Jay's room and the boy in Jake's room. This was of course before Jake's romantic attention turned toward men.

We never knew who might be spending the night on the couch or on an air mattress in the family room. There was always a friend or two spending the night, often kids who had gotten into a fight with their parents and had nowhere else to go. Sometimes they'd stay for a night, sometimes for weeks. All of Jake and Jay's friends knew where they could go to find a warm bed and a hot meal if needed. I never knew who would be here in the morning when I woke up. There would be kids strewn all over the house. I'd walk out in the morning and see hands and feet hanging over the edge of every couch and love seat. I enjoyed having the house full of young people. It was a special time.

We experienced many unusual situations that made us chuckle. Once Jake, who had started the transition and looked like a male but had not yet legally changed his gender and name, went to pick up a prescription at the pharmacy in Julia's name. The pharmacy technician commented how sweet it was that a big brother was picking up a prescription for his sister. Jake's response was, "Yeah, right." I remember when our old exterminator returned after working in another area for five years. He had known Jake as Julia and hadn't seen any of us during the time when Jake was going through the transition. He came inside to do an inspection and noticed my picture gallery of the kids at various stages of their lives. He furrowed his brow, looked again and seemed puzzled. He turned to me and said, "I don't mean to be too personal, but don't you also have a daughter?" I replied, "I did," and left it at that. My response probably didn't clear things up for him. He probably walked away thinking something horrible had happened to my daughter and never inquired again.

The elderly neighbor next door had been very friendly with my kids for years and did nice things when they were little like bringing them cupcakes for Halloween. I hadn't seen her for a while. After Jake's transition, she assumed he was Jay. She asked me one day, "Where's Julia? I haven't seen her in a long time?" Because she was older and I didn't want to start a lengthy conversation, I answered, "Oh, she's away at college." At some point I did explain the situation to her because she continued to call Jake by his brother's name. I'm not sure if she ever really understood.

Once when we were leaving to go on a Caribbean vacation, Jake had trouble with security at the airport because the name on his driver's license did not match the name on his airline ticket and he no longer looked like the picture on his driver's license. We didn't think about this until we got to the airport and worried that they wouldn't let Jake on the plane. Luckily, since he was still a minor, they did eventually let him through. Which was a good thing since I was not about to leave Jake home alone and I certainly was not going to forego my greatly needed vacation.

Following our uncomfortable experience at the airport, I realized it was time to change the name and gender on Jake's legal documents from Julia to Jake. Legally changing his name and gender was an involved process. I researched online how to do it. I thought, "How hard could it be?" Well, after my third trip to the courthouse, with my paperwork still incomplete, I realized it wasn't as easy as I thought it would be. That's why people consult with lawyers.

Thankfully, the Transgender Law Center in San Francisco was very helpful.[1] I was directed to the court website, where I was able to download the necessary forms for legal gender change and legal name change. It seems I always do things twice as hard as is necessary. I didn't realize you could apply for a gender and a name change on the same form. Instead I filled out two separate forms. I completed the paperwork and took it to the courthouse, where I waited in line (the first time...). When I got to the window, the clerk told me the paperwork all looked fine except for one thing. Evidently I needed to include the language "specify through her guardian" because Jake was a minor. I took care of that, then the form was stamped and we were given a court date. We were sent to another office upstairs, where they gave us yet another form to fill out, a petition for change of gender. The hearing was set for February 15, 2008.

The gender and name change process is not cheap. The cost was between $500 and $600 just to file the forms with the county clerk's office. They did a background check to see if Jake had a criminal record, which of course he did not. Finally, we appeared before a judge, who read through the paperwork. The judge had never presided over a gender change before and

---

1   www.transgenderlawcenter.org

wasn't really sure how to do it. I actually had to walk him through it. I explained, "We're changing his name and gender because he's transgender." The judge asked me, "Are you sure this is all the paperwork that needs to be done?" I assured him it was. He replied, "Okay, I'll take your word for it." Really? That's the blind leading the blind. The judge asked Jake a few questions, seemed satisfied, then approved and stamped the documents.

The paperwork went back to the clerk's office to be filed. It was officially filed in October, and that's when Jake's name and gender legally changed. We had to obtain certified copies of the original "order to change name and gender," to use as proof that his name and gender had been legally changed whenever we needed to adjust additional legal documents. Next on our agenda was to have his name and gender marker corrected on his driver's license.

We completed the necessary paperwork at the Department of Motor Vehicles (DMV) and, at that time, had to show proof from one of the doctors treating Jake that he had gone through the process of medically transitioning. The endocrinologist wrote a letter verifying that Jake had been his patient since October 2006, had been diagnosed with gender identity disorder (now called gender dysphoria) and had begun HRT in November of 2006. In addition, it verified that Jake had a gender-defining surgical correction in January of 2007. The doctor concluded that Jake had successfully transitioned to male and verified that he had supported the transition.

Primary sex characteristics are our internal body parts. The term "secondary sex characteristics" refers to your external body parts and how you present to the world. At that time, transitioning required either the removal or addition of a secondary sex characteristic, (i.e., penis or breasts). When transitioning from female to male, there are surgical techniques available to transform female genitalia to male genitalia. These surgical procedures have come a long way, but they haven't been entirely perfected and are extremely expensive, and not without risk. At that time, to be considered legally transitioned and eligible for a legal gender and name change, you must have undergone some sort of secondary sex characteristic alteration. The language "had gender defining surgical correction" meant in Jake's case that he had had a double mastectomy (aka chest reconstruction). That was necessary lingo in the paperwork and something I became aware of while doing the research.

Since that time, the standards of care have changed. The Vital Statistics Modernization Act, passed in March of 2011, clarifies the documentation and residency requirements for obtaining a California court-ordered gender change. This law clarifies that both individuals born in California and individuals who currently reside in California may petition a California court for a gender change. In addition, the Act changes the documentation standard for obtaining a legal gender change in California from "surgery that changes sex characteristics" to "clinically appropriate treatment for the purposes of gender transition."[2]

---

2   www.transgenderlawcenter.org

After the name and gender changes were made official and Jake became an 18-year-old man, he received a request to register for selective service. Now this was something we hadn't anticipated. This brought up a lot of new concerns. How would they handle my transgender son in the military? Would he be safe? As we read down the list of individuals who would be exempt from registering for the military, such as "already in the military" and "medical issues," I was relieved to see that the very last category was "transsexual." Jake checked off the box and indicated that at birth his gender was female. He was required to attach a copy of his original birth certificate. Jake received a letter back that said, "Based on the records and information you provided, you are not required to register." It's not that I don't support and respect our military. I absolutely do. It's what keeps our borders safe and our country free. Furthermore, my father was a captain in the U.S. Navy. But Jake, in the military? That was not something I could imagine. I love him to death but I'm sure he'd shoot himself in the foot.

The ban on transgender persons in the military, which had been in place for decades, was based on the outdated diagnosis of transgender as a psychiatric disorder. It was also due to fears that, according to President Elaine Donnelly of the Center for Military Readiness:

> putting transgender people in barracks, showers and other sex-segregated facilities could cause sexual assaults to increase and infringe on the privacy of non-transgender personnel. This is putting an extra

burden on men and women in the military that they certainly don't need and don't deserve.[3]

As of July 2015, this ban was overturned. Twelve months later, Defense Secretary Ash Carter announced, "Effective immediately, transgender Service members may serve openly, and they can no longer be discharged or otherwise separated from the military solely for being transgender individuals."[4]

Julia legally became Jacob. We discovered that it's harder to get a passport with a gender and name change than a driver's license, due to national security concerns and identity theft. Since the terrorist attacks on 9/11, it's harder for anyone to get a passport or a birth certificate. The government puts you through a lot to make sure you are not stealing someone else's identity. Again, I got a wealth of useful information from the Transgender Law Center. We had to change the name on Jake's social security card. There was a lot more paperwork involved to substantiate Jake's transition. We had to provide certified copies of the court orders that approved the name and gender change. To allow your child to do something like this is quite a commitment, financially, legally, and personally. It's also a time commitment if you choose to do it, like I did, on your own.

After Jake started college and had moved out, we started having a family movie night. We'd arrange the couches for the three couples—my husband and me,

---

3 Leff, L. (2014) "APNewsBreak: Transgender troop ban faces scrutiny." *Huffington Post, March 13.* Accessed on 21/01/17 at www. huffingtonpost.com/huff-wires/20140313/us-transgender-miitary-service/?utm_hp_ref=politics&ir=politics

4 www.defense.gov/news/specialreports/0616_transgender-policy

Jake, Jay, and their respective boyfriends. Izzy and I would shake our heads and laugh. Here we were, such proud parents, watching a movie and eating popcorn with our sons and their significant others. We couldn't help but imagine that this would not be as acceptable in some other households as it was in ours. After all we had weathered, it felt so nice to be a close family again.

22

THE ZEN OF DUCKS

—— (2014–Present Day) ——

I'm hiking in the canyon with a close friend, a former Buddhist nun. I consider her one of my spiritual guides, someone who taught me to be present and non-judgmental. We finish our hike and take our usual rest at a picnic table by the duck pond. It's a beautiful spring day, sunny and crisp. It's mid-week and no other people are around. My friend closes her eyes to meditate. As I meditate with my eyes open, I take in the natural beauty of the setting. Watching the turtles, ducks, and birds, I observe a fish glide by beneath the surface of the pond.

I really concentrate on the sounds of the animals and the wind blowing, and feel connected to everything around me. Suddenly I see a duckling. It seems to be trapped in a hidden area surrounded by tall reeds of grass. I watch it, trying to figure out what it's going to do. The duck starts to make a noise, more of a chirp than a quack. In the distance I hear the quack of an older duck. Glancing in that direction, I see a larger duck in the middle of the pond, swimming erratically, and looking around. It keeps quacking, as if answering the call of the duckling. The younger bird chirps back.

They are talking to one another. The larger duck, the mother, reaches the reeds, pushes them back with her body, and looks in the opening. The baby peeps. The mother comes rushing in to rescue her. They intertwine their beaks, like they are kissing each other. They seem to greet each other with relief and joy.

The mother escorts the duckling to a safe place. I hear no more chirping, no more quacking. Seconds later, I see the mother duck swimming across the pond to a bushy area, with a long reed of dried grass in her mouth. She swims across the pond, under some branches and dips into the water. I see her emerge a few seconds later without the reed. The mother duck darts back across the pond, grabs another reed, takes it to the nest she is building, then repeats this several more times. As I am watching this, I feel myself becoming very emotional, and my eyes fill with tears. What I have witnessed seems so amazing, so incredible. "Look at the mommy duck. It comes when her baby calls. She leads it to safety, then goes back to building their home."

I suddenly realize that for my entire life that's all I ever wanted, my mother to be there for me. But she never was. That's what my journey has been all about— finding a home. Being there for my ducklings, coming when they call me and need me, leading them to safety, teaching them how to take care of themselves, and making a nice home for them. Then, when they are ready, being able to let them fly out of the nest and build their own lives, with the awareness that I'll always be there for them and have their back.

Even though it sometimes feels like I was raised by wolves, I often ask myself, "How did I miraculously figure out how to be a halfway decent mother, negotiate the unexpected twists and turns of our unique ride, and wind up with such amazing children?" The short answer is, it was a long journey and it wasn't easy. It starts with how I formulated my philosophy of life, which gives me the strength to get through my own personal traumas, enables me to be a strong, loving, and supportive mom, and shows me the light that leads my sons out of their darkest hours, helping them to become productive and happy young adults.

I hated how negative my adoptive mother Joan could be. But, because I was exposed to her pessimism for so many years, some of it unfortunately rubbed off on me. However, my negativity was different than hers, it was more akin to envy. I was envious of what I perceived to be other people's happiness and peacefulness, their more "normal" family, and having loving parents. My father was not a negative person, he never said a nasty word about anyone. He was a humanistic man, very involved in our community, and the opposite of my mom. However, he was emotionally unavailable.

My mother was resentful of everyone else's happiness, but would not allow herself to be happy. Dad provided a nice life for her and it was sad that she never could appreciate it. This goes to show that true happiness comes from within. Mom died a miserable woman. She never found internal peace or self-love. That's why I started my spiritual quest. I knew that all the tangible items in the world would not give me inner peace. I struggled to really know myself. I forced myself to feel my pain and sit in the discomfort so I could work through it to truly get to the depths of my inner soul. I did whatever I could to avoid emulating my mother.

Dad may not have been able to connect emotionally, but he was always available for an intellectual conversation. When I was around ten years old I remember asking my dad if he believed in ghosts. I didn't fear ghosts, but... Grandma had antiques. I inherited my grandmother's four-poster bed after my grandfather died. The bed was high up with a space underneath. As a kid, I feared something might be lurking under the bed. I asked my dad if he believed in ghosts.

Since dad was a physicist, most every explanation he had was based on science. So of course his answer to my ethereal question began with a quote from Albert Einstein. "Energy cannot be created nor destroyed, it can only be changed from one form to another." My father elaborated by saying, "The human body is made up of matter and energy, and since energy can neither be created nor destroyed, when the host of the energy dies, the energy leaves the host and travels somewhere else. Could the traveling energy be a ghost? Possibly. That which can't be proven, can't be disproven either." Dad had studied so much about metaphysical topics. In his search for knowledge, he read everything from the Kabala to Einstein. His conclusion was, "You never know." If you can't definitively say yes or no, then it's possible. Even though dad's answer to my ghost question was a complicated physics explanation, it made sense and was comforting to me. But the humorous part was, at that age, all I really wanted was a "Yes" or "No" answer.

My need for spiritual enlightenment grew as I encountered more challenges in my life. I was always searching for an answer as to why life had to be so difficult and a way to achieve some inner peace. My hiking friend introduced me to the principles of Buddhism, which spoke to me. What appeals to me about Buddhism is the introspection through meditation, staying present, trying to be as non-judgmental as possible, and breathing. I don't aspire to be a full Buddhist, but I incorporate many Buddhist ideals in my personal spiritual belief system and practice. This has enabled me to better embrace life and experience the full range of human emotions. I have to feel pain to be able to enjoy pleasure, I need to experience sadness in order to know what happiness is, and it's important for me to recognize the thin line between love and hate in order to have true, honest relationships.

My spiritual quest has been about learning to be able to sit with myself, to accept myself, to be a better person, mother, wife, therapist, child, and friend. Reaching a place of self-acceptance and self-compassion has been really life changing for me. I've been trying to pass this philosophy on to my children. Someone once asked Jake what religion he follows, and I was touched when he responded, "I'm a 'BuJew' just like my mom."

My philosophy has helped me get through everything that has happened in my 50-plus years. I have learned to put my expectations aside and take life as it comes. A true Buddhist might believe that his pain and suffering is a reflection of something he did in a past life. But I believe that the sad and uncomfortable events of my life have had nothing to do with what I did or didn't do. It just is what it is.

There were moments when it felt like I was losing it. I was distraught, helpless, lost, hadn't found resources yet, or learned how to advocate and help Jake or Jay. I just felt their pain. I've learned we're only as happy as our unhappiest child. Meditation, sitting still, breathing, taking a moment to be in the moment, to not have my head spinning, not going through my list of "What ifs," not catastrophizing, really helped. Meditating anywhere from a few minutes to an hour gave me the time I needed to ground myself. I realized that I had to learn how to be in the moment and deal with whatever came, one thing at a time. I had to stay present and focused for my kids. If I had fallen apart, who would take care of them? My husband couldn't at first. He backed off, couldn't face it and got angry. It was traumatic for all of us. I had to go within to find the strength. And I did.

I became proactive and started working on the problem as opposed to asking why and praying for it to be over. Before I knew it we were on a path to healing, moving forward, and not giving up. Never give up. I helped Jake and later Jay become hopeful. Once they became hopeful, we became a team and helped each other. In the beginning, Izzy blamed me. For instance, he thought I shouldn't have let Jake hang out with "strange" people. He wanted to blame someone. I knew intellectually, from my medical research, that Jake's situation was biological. It wasn't my fault. Both Jake and Jay's emotional stability and ability to be successful would be my fault if I hadn't backed them up and been their support system.

The message I want parents to receive is that we play a huge part in our children's happiness. If we have rigid expectations of our children following a straight and narrow path, and fitting into a socially conforming mold, we are doing them an injustice. It's our job to give our children, no matter who they are or who they love, a foundation in life, to teach them healthy values, and guide them on the path to becoming compassionate, productive members of society.

Today, when I see Jake's compassion and respect for other people, his ability to lead meetings for his organization, being able to get up in front of thousands of people and give an acceptance speech, or just walking down the street knowing who he is and what he's been through, he just amazes me. My younger son Jay, who has struggled with OCD and an eating disorder, equally impresses me. I am grateful that, considering all their challenges, they made it this far and did not succumb to alcoholism, drug addiction, or suicide as a way of coping, as others have done.

Both my sons are now in their mid-20s. Both are college graduates and live on their own. Jay received his undergraduate degree in screenwriting and now works as a freelance screenwriter and script editor. Jake earned his undergraduate degree in psychology, and is currently attending graduate school where he is working towards a degree in clinical psychology with a specialization in LGBT affirming psychology. They both have a large group of supportive friends and continue to negotiate intimate relationships.

Jake and Jay live nearby and I feel fortunate that I can see them regularly. I consider our family close knit. Typical of siblings, my sons get along the majority of the time but occasionally quarrel. Sure, sometimes I want to throttle them, but no one is perfect and I usually refrain from the impulse. I have learned how important it is to pick my battles. Both of my young men have adopted philosophies similar to mine, are good human beings, and have respect for other people.

I believe we are all continuous "works in progress." It is important to have compassion for ourselves as well as the willingness to see our own need for personal growth. My life experiences have helped to fill my toolbox with parenting skills. I love my boys with all my heart and I am proud to be their mother.

FURTHER READING

American Psychiatric Association (APA) (2013) *Diagnostic and Statistical Manual of Mental Disorders*, 5th edn. Washington, DC: American Psychiatric Association.

Brill, S., and Pepper, R. (2008) *The Transgender Child: A Handbook for Families and Professionals*. Jersey City, NJ: Cleis Press.

Flores, A.R., Herman, J.L., Gates, G.J., and Brown, T.N.T. (2016) *How Many Adults Identify as Transgender in the United States?* Los Angeles, CA: The Williams Institute.

Grahl, G.A. (2007) *Skinny Boy*. Clearfield, UT: American Legacy Media.

Green, J. (2004) *Becoming a Visible Man*. Nashville, TN: Vanderbilt University Press.

Hubbard, E.A., and Whitley, C.T. (2012) *Trans-Kin: A Guide for Family & Friends of Transgender People*. Boulder, CO: Bolder Press.

Roth, K., Friedman, F.B., and Kreger, R. (2003) *Surviving a Borderline Parent: How to Heal Your Childhood Wounds & Build Trust, Boundaries and Self-Esteem*. Oakland, CA: New Harbinger Publications.

Savin-Williams, R. (2005) *The New Gay Teenager*. Cambridge, MA: Harvard University Press.

Wolf, A. (2002) *Get Out of My Life, but First Could You Drive Me and Cheryl to the Mall?* New York: Farrar, Straus and Giroux.

RESOURCES

Children's Hospital Los Angeles
Center for Transyouth Health and Development
Provides hormonal intervention, mental health, health education, peer support, and advocacy services for transgender youth, and consultation for families with gender non-conforming children.

5000 Sunset Boulevard, 4th floor
Los Angeles, California 90027

Phone: 323-361-5372
E-mail: jjulian@chla.usc.edu

Gender Odyssey
An annual conference for professionals and families that offers over 70 informative and empowering workshops, films, receptions, performances, and the chance to make lifelong friends.

6523 California Avenue SW, #360
Seattle, Washington 98136

E-mail: info@genderodyssey.org

www.genderodyssey.org

Gender Spectrum
Provides an array of services to help youth, families, organizations, and institutions understand and address concepts of gender identity and gender expression.

Phone: 510-788-4412
E-mail: info@genderspectrum.org

www.genderspectrum.org

Los Angeles LGBT Center

Provides services for more LGBT people than any organization in the world. Offering programs, services, and global advocacy that span four broad categories: health, social services and housing, culture and education, leadership and advocacy.

McDonald/Wright Building
1625 North Schrader Boulevard
Los Angeles, California 90028-6213

Phone: 323-993-7400

www.lalgbtcenter.org

Mazzoni Center

Provides quality comprehensive health and wellness services in an LGBTQ-focused environment, while preserving the dignity and improving the quality of life of the individuals they serve.
Main offices: 21 South 12th Street, 8th Floor
Philadelphia, Pennsylvania 19107

Phone: 215-563-0652
Fax: 215-563-0664
Legal services: 215-563-0657

www.mazzonicenter.org

St John's Well Child and Family Center

Welcomes all patients regardless of gender identity, sexual orientation, and/or presentation. Provides comprehensive health services in a safe and welcoming environment where you are free to be yourself.

80 West 58th Street
Los Angeles, California 90037

Phone: 323-541-1600
Fax: 323-541-1661
E-mail: info@wellchild.org

www.wellchild.org

TransActive Gender Center

Provides a holistic range of services and expertise to empower transgender and gender diverse children, youth, and their families in living healthy lives, free of discrimination.

1631 NE Broadway Street #355-T
Portland, Oregon 97232

Phone: 503-252-3000
Fax: 503-255-3367
E-mail: info@transactiveonline.org

Transgender Law Center

Works to change law, policy, and attitudes so that all people can live safely, authentically, and free from discrimination regardless of their gender identity or expression.

PO Box 70976
Oakland, California 94612-0976

Phone: 510-587-9696
Collect line for inmates & detainees: 510-380-8229
Fax: 877-847-1278

www.transgenderlawcenter.org

Trans United with Family and Friends (TUFF)

Dedicated to helping ease the financial burden of underserved trans individuals, to ease their access to healthcare, transition services, safe housing, and education.

E-mail: tufforg@gmail.com

www.tufforg.com

The World Professional Association for Transgender Health (WPATH)

To promote evidence-based care, education, research, advocacy, public policy, and respect in transgender health.

www.wpath.org